Rose Growing for Everyone

by the same author
ROSE GROWING COMPLETE

E. B. Le GRICE

Rose Growing
for Everyone

FABER AND FABER
24 Russell Square
London

First published in 1969
by Faber and Faber Limited
24 Russell Square London WC1
Printed in Great Britain by
Latimer Trend & Co Ltd Plymouth
All rights reserved

SBN 571 08682 9

LINE DRAWINGS BY
RUTH EDWARDS

© 1969 by E. B. Le Grice

To the beginner—
the expert of the future

Contents

Introduction *page* 13

PART I: THE ROOT

1. Planning and Preparation 17
2. Planting 29
3. Cultivation and Manuring 38

PART II: THE SHOOT

4. Pruning 47
5. After-care: Pests and Diseases 65
6. Afterthoughts: Training, Staking and Tying; Hedges 74

PART III: THE FLOWER AND THE BUSH

7. Rose Blooms: How to Identify and Treat Them 87
8. Choosing Your Rose Bushes 99
9. Group 1: Ramblers and Climbers 105
10. Group 2: Old-Fashioned Roses, Species and Shrubs 115
11. Group 3: The Floribunda Roses 120
12. Group 4: Hybrid Tea Roses 131

Appendix: Selections for various purposes 143
Index 145

Illustrations

PLATES

COLOUR

An arrangement of mixed roses   *facing page* 12

MONOCHROME

1 (a).	Black Spot	64
(b).	Rust	64
2 (a).	Mildew	65
(b).	Aphides	65
(c).	Larvae of leaf rooling sawfly	65
3.	Maigold (Perpetual Rambler)	80
4.	Albertine Rambler	81
5.	Rosa gallica versicolor (Rosa Mundi)	112
6.	Rosa Filipes 'Kiftsgate'	113
7 (a).	Superior (floribunda)	128
(b).	Goldgleam (floribunda)	128
8 (a).	Virgo (H.T.)	129
(b).	Pink Favourite (H.T.)	129

The colour plate and plate 7a are reproduced by courtesy of J. E. Downward; plates 7b, 8a and 8b by courtesy of Charles E. Mace, A.M.P.A.; plates 1a and b, 2a, b and c by courtesy of Murphy Chemical Company Ltd.; and plate 6 by courtesy of Mrs. Jocelyn Steward.

ILLUSTRATIONS

LINE DRAWINGS

1. Diagrams of plant and flower — page 18
2. Digging the new bed — 26
3. Planting — 31
4. Resuscitating very dry plants — 33
5. Heeling in — 34
6. Hilling up — 35
7. Watering a climber or rambler planted against a wall — 36
8. Suckering — 42
9. Pruning an old neglected bush — 52
10. Pruning cuts: wrong and right — 53
11. 'Summer Pruning' — 55
12. Training of climbers and ramblers — 57
13. Pruning polyantha and floribunda roses — 61
14. Pruning H.T. roses — 63
15. Standard rose tree and Weeping standard — 77
16. Flower head of floribunda type — 92
17. Flower head of H.T. type — 93
18. Minimum standards for rose plants — 100–2

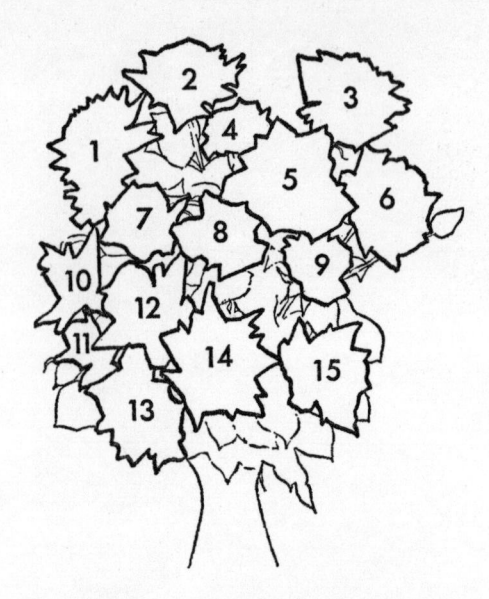

		Raiser	*Grower and Country*
1	**My Choice**	Le Grice	E. B. Le Grice, England
2	**Thais**	Meilland	Universal Rose Selection, France
3	**Incense**	Le Grice	E. B. Le Grice, England
4	**Femina**	Gaujard	Jean Gaujard, France
5	**Vienna Charm**	Kordes	R. Kordes, Germany
6	**Gavotte**	Sanday	John Sanday (Roses) Ltd, England
7	**Message**	Meilland	Universal Rose Selection, France
8	**King's Ransome**	Morrey	Dennison Morrey, U.S.A.
9	**Ellen Mary**	Le Grice	E. B. Le Grice, England
10	**Grandpa Dickson**	Dickson	A. R. C. Dickson, Ireland
11	**Ernest H. Morse**	Kordes	R. Kordes, Germany
12	**Mischief**	McGredy	S. McGredy, Ireland
13	**Chicago Peace**	Johnston	E. Johnston, U.S.A.
14	**Diorama**	De Ruiter	G. De Ruiter, Holland
15	**Wendy Cussons**	Gregory	C. W. Gregory & Son, England

An arrangement of mixed roses

Introduction

Foundations are of the utmost importance whether it be the Forth Bridge, a well-dressed lady or a healthy rose bush. It is only because the unseen has been carefully prepared that the visible effect, whether it be for utility or pleasure, achieves its purpose. This is fully true of the rose bush. Because the root, unseen and unsung, is so vital to the well-being of the whole plant it has been given the first section in a book written with beginners especially in mind. Because there are tens of thousands of new homes spreading across a vast acreage of the English countryside and because there are so many happy couples setting up home for the first time each year, this book is prepared for such. Gardening may be an adventure into a new experience, a great thrill, a journey of a lifetime. This book is a chart, a road map where the main highways most generally used are depicted. This is no hiker's map to lead you into the delightful byways reserved for the experienced few, but it is designed to map out an area of knowledge in which you cannot go astray, and which although it may be enlarged by further experience will not have to be unlearned later.

It is my hope that having travelled these main routes so that you know the major rules of rose growing well, you may be induced to traverse the byways of the specialist and become not only a grower of roses but a lover of the craft, so that leaving uncertain experiment behind you

INTRODUCTION

may strike out into the new adventure encouraged by the success of earlier experience.

As a child of twelve trying to grow my first rose trees I learned by bitter failure that enthusiasm is no substitute for experience. As a callow youth I learned from the knowledge of those who had grown rose-wise by generations of practice. In maturity I would share with you the delights of a lifetime spent in rose growing among those who have grown older, wiser and more kindly in their pastime or profession.

PART I
The Root

I

Planning and Preparation

We must think of the rose bush as having three important parts, the roots, the branches and finally the bush with its flowers. They must be considered in that order, and only when we have good roots doing their work well can the branches function, and only when there is a happy balance between root and branch can the end product, the flowering bush, flourish as we should like.

This is why it is so important to get a good plant having a strong, vigorous root system, for this is essential if its work is to be done satisfactorily.

The root (see fig. 1) has three main functions. The first is to provide anchorage. We need a bush which can withstand strain and carry a heavy top without collapsing, especially when the plant, weighted with rain-soaked flower and foliage, has to withstand a summer gale. The second function is to draw up moisture, which depends largely upon the same type of root—those deep, thrusting, coarse roots which delve into the subsoil and because of their depth can draw up water even in a time of drought. It is their strength and ability to enter the subsoil which enables the plant to continue growth during dry weather. The third function devolves upon a different type of root. This is the fibre—fine roots in a heavy network quite near the soil surface. It is through the tips of these fine roots that food passes into the plant. They are of the greatest importance and their encouragement, protection and nourishment should be the first consideration of the keen

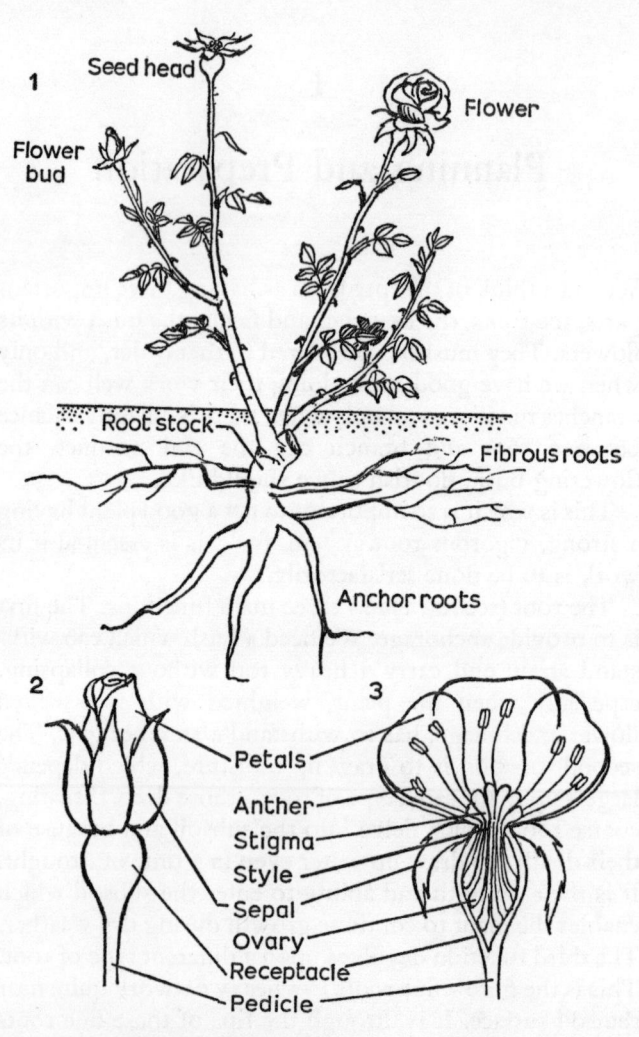

1. (1) Diagram of the plant
   (2) The parts of the flower
   (3) Section of flower, showing structure

plantsman. Roots are of two kinds on the best rose trees. Deep roots to anchor and draw up water, fine roots through which the plant is fed. The deep roots are permanent, but the fibrous roots are being renewed continually.

We shall come back to the root and see where this knowledge leads us. A very common fault is to forget that the most important part of the plant is 'out of sight'. It behoves us to see that it is not 'out of mind'!

The root, important as it is, can fulfil its function only if the shoot (see diagram) above it is doing its assigned task. The shoot has an important work which varies with the duty it has to perform. It may be short and sturdy, tall and branching or slender and far reaching. Even so, there are general characteristics common to all. The shoot is the framework for leaves, flower and fruit. It needs enough rigidity to fulfil its purpose. It has to carry spaced leaves which depend upon light, air and moisture to manufacture the source of energy for the plant. The stem is needed to carry the water to the leaf and to act as transport canals so that the foods in the plant may be carried where they are needed and, if there is a surplus, to store this until it is required. The stem must also carry the flower so that it may attract insects for fertilization and when fertilized produce seed. This last function of the flower is its natural purpose. Man-produced varieties may defeat nature by doubling the flower or producing infertile flowers and pollen, for man's object is an unnatural one as far as the fertility of the rose is concerned. Man seeks to prevent seeding for a variety of reasons which will be explained later.

Consider for a moment the cycle in the plant's life. The rose is part of the family Rosaceae to which belong a very wide variety of plants, including fruits such as apples, ornamental shrubs such as potentillas and an amazing number of types. In nearly all cases they are deciduous.

THE ROOT

This is a word generally used in horticulture to describe plants which at some resting period of the plant shed their leaves. This natural occurrence has caused serious concern to beginners and I have had customers ring me up in great alarm to tell me that the roses planted a few days before are dying. 'Their leaves are shrivelling and falling off.' This is really a natural and fortunate occurrence, for it gives a dormant period in the plant's life cycle so that the very delicate operation of transplanting may be carried out with success. Transplanting a rose is like carrying out an operation on a human patient under an anaesthetic. It needs to be performed speedily and efficiently and this demands previous planning and preparation.

In the wild state the genus *rosa* is very widely distributed over all the Northern Hemisphere and has adapted itself to a great variety of climates. Some species can stand bitter cold, others enjoy sub-tropical temperatures. Some types will withstand drought, others are used to abundant moisture. It is in the great variety of forms that roses excel. From low creeping plants a few inches high to rampant climbers sprawling for 40 feet. From sturdy thorny bushes to lanky, almost thornless, shrubs. Many produce impenetrable thickets which throw up shoots at a distance from the mother plant. These 'suckers', as they are called, may invade wide areas.

To bring all this variety into the confines of a suburban garden would be impossible. The hybridist has for his object the production of plants possessing the best characters of the wild roses consistent with his purpose, which is ever the maximum decoration in a minimum of ordered space.

As we deal with types of plants these will be described by their salient features so that you, the reader, may recognize them and know their uses and employ them for your special purpose (see pages 89–94).

PLANNING AND PREPARATION

Bearing these preliminary remarks in mind we will begin where many new gardeners have to start. The tangled jungle left by the builder, or worse, the wilderness left by the bulldozer. In either case the first consideration must be the soil and its preparation. To understand this we must think of the site and its aspect.

Ideally we would have some choice in this matter but usually our living or other pressing responsibilities determine where we should live. If we had the choice the site would be open so that the air could circulate freely, and the larger part of the garden would be on a gentle slope facing south or south-west so that the sunshine could play upon our plants throughout the day. If we cannot choose the site for our garden we can usually plant our bushes where they will get the maximum of sun and air which the position can afford. 'Air' should not be confused with a draught, that chilly cutting blast which is the forerunner of mildew.

We may usually expect the soil to be one of three main types. 'Heavy', a term used for soil containing a preponderance of clay, which, because of its fine particles, fails to drain well. This type is the most difficult to make workable, but may be improved by deep (20 in.) digging, adding dry peat of a coarse nature which may be scattered to a depth of 4 in. on the surface and then, as digging proceeds, worked into all the soil as it is turned over. It is useless to excavate a bed and fill with more kindly earth as the moisture will seep in from the surrounding soil and make a pit of the new bed. If you have the money, spend it on getting the land well broken over the whole area and put down to grass, bringing a portion only into cultivation as time and circumstances permit. If drainage is needed, then get an expert to advise you. 'Heavy' land means hard work, but being richer in plant foods it will, when reduced from savagery, yield excellent results. It is a fallacy to think that roses 'like heavy soil'. They don't need it and you will not want it, although with care excellent growth and good flowers will result.

After 'heavy' comes 'loam', which should suit every Englishman, who is supposed to be a master of compromise. Here we have 50 per cent clay and 50 per cent sand, so drainage in these circumstances is easy, but the food content is still good. Such soil can be worked without undue manual strain and amply repays care and effort.

The third main type is 'light' land, where sand predominates. This should never deter anyone. Such land is easy to work and responds to careful treatment, and can be greatly rewarding if fed generously and regularly with the right materials. The right materials are of two kinds and will be dealt with under feeding, but the main concern of the beginner will be to get the right stuff in the right place. The lower soil can be treated once only—when the bed is being made. Success lies in abundant 'humus'—vegetable matter in varying states of decay. Farmyard manure, well rotted, is the ideal, but failing this, ample peat or a good compost is essential. The object is less that of feeding the plant and more of providing the right soil texture, to make the soil more spongy so that moisture may be retained and air circulation made possible. Airless soil is as unhealthy as an airless environment above ground. Once your garden is established and your experience widened the making of compost should provide excellent humus of the best sort, but 'compost' is not stinking decaying refuse such as a heap of rotting grass mowings. It is a pleasant, easily handled, well-balanced vegetable base carefully prepared, which demands care and skill. Few materials are such great assets to good gardening, but compost making is a skill to be learned.[1]

A type presenting a problem is the very stony soil which

---

[1] See *Rose Growing Complete*, pp. 37–39.

PLANNING AND PREPARATION

may contain large stones or even small rocks. It is well to remember that stones are natural to such soils and often provide essential drainage. On the other hand big stones occupy valuable space needed for fertile soil. Common sense is needed. Remove the largest stones even down to 1–1½ in. in diameter, but do not sift the earth. The removal of all stone would make the last state worse than the first.

There are other types which are less amenable. Those where the top earth is shallow and where chalk, gravel or other infertile substances are near the surface. In such cases it may be necessary to take out the material present to a depth of 18 in. and refill with good earth, always bearing in mind that good drainage is essential throughout the whole plot. This is a costly and time-consuming task, but better to grow a few bushes well than have a large number of ailing specimens.

This is a principle which should be kept in mind. If you are a novice 'make haste slowly'. Prepare a small bed thoroughly, plant a few good roses well and success will soon demand an increase. Do not be in so much of a hurry that your first harvest is discouragement.

It should be a punishable offence for the land grabber to neglect the housing site so that the purchaser inherits an accumulation of weeds and seed which could have been prevented at little extra cost while the land was being converted from farm land to homestead. If it is your lot to inherit such land then give at least a season of preparation before planting. A spring and summer spent in clearing and cleaning the land will return a future harvest of carefree cultivation.

There are many aids to cultivation when land is clear of plants and paths. It is possible in some cases to have the site ploughed. If this is done it should be done well with a reversible single furrow plough. Usually the site is not sufficiently accessible once building begins, but if this can be done once the site of the house has been settled and the garden marked off so that it can remain untouched, then the soil will never be as compacted again and future digging or cultivation can be done more easily and speedily.

It is possible to hire mechanical hand cultivators and it is better to hire. These are expensive machines and a breakdown of a loan from a friend when it is in use may place one under an obligation to repair it which can be very costly. Little ploughs are not much good, they cannot till the land deeply enough, but rotovators which break up the soil finely will soften the top soil, cut up the weeds and enable deeper cultivation to be carried out more easily.

Very great care should be used with weed-killing sprays and expert advice should be sought, as they are highly selective, needing special sprays for different weeds.

There are general rules which may well be followed under most conditions and while these may need minor adaptations the main principles are the same.

The first demand should be to plan the site. Do this as a whole. Do not dump a dozen roses in a scratched-out hole and attempt to build a garden round them. Plan the whole site. Draw a plan, noting the slope of the land, any irregularities which may need levelling and consider your personal needs. Will you later require a tool shed, a garage or a short cut to the gate when you have a bus to catch? If you begin a plan before the house is built do not consider this as final. No plan should be considered as complete until the owners have stood within the house and viewed the garden from the windows. Most of one's life, especially the wife's, will be spent in the kitchen or living-room looking out into the garden. That is why a plan should be finalized after the house is built.

PLANNING AND PREPARATION

It may be a long while before the garden is finished but it should be regarded as a whole. It is a blessing that rose trees yield returns quickly so that the open scars of fresh building may be healed in a short time. Make your beds for roses as large as you can within the framework you have planned. Better one bed containing twenty-four rose trees than four beds of six each. So much unnecessary work is saved.

If you consider your garden too small for a separate bed—and very few are—then specimen bushes planted singly or in small groups can be very effective. Edges are always a problem, and the length of these should be cut to a minimum. If you have a driveway make the drive one edge of your bed. The hard straight line can always be softened by careful planting.

For the beginner, simple designs with square, oblong or circular beds will be advisable. Crescents, undulations and ovals are more difficult to design and keep in order.

After planning comes the preparation and this is the crucial phase of the whole procedure. Do NOT scamp the work. If you are in an office and have a week off do not spend it all on heavy slogging. You will probably crawl to the doctor before the week is out with lumbago! Be prepared for hard work, but not for work outside your capacity.

Usually it is better first to mark out the bed or beds with string. Then tackle each bed by removing the first trench for the width of the bed, if narrow, or half the bed if it is wide (see fig. 2). By removing the first 'spit' (section of earth a spade wide and a spade deep, i.e. 10 in. × 10 in.) a trench will be opened. Cover this trench with 3 in. of peat and 2 oz. of bonemeal each foot run, for this is the only time you will be able to feed the deep soils. Then fork this in as deeply as possible, which will probably be about 8 in. This will give a total depth of 18 in. in which

THE ROOT

the roots will find sufficient room to make good growth. Only under exceptional soil conditions should deeper digging be necessary. If the bed is wide (see below, fig. 2)

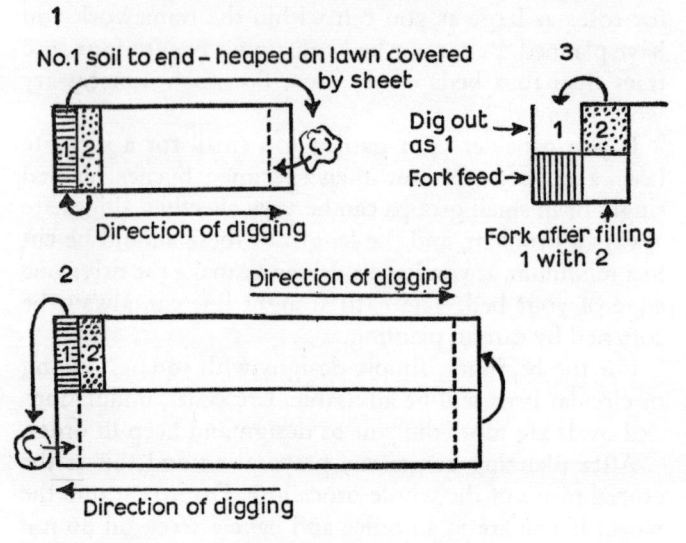

2. Digging the new bed

it may be divided lengthwise into two strips, and the first trench made will supply the soil needed to fill in the empty trench left at the end of digging. The soil may be piled near the end of the bed just beyond its limits. A narrow bed may need to have the soil surplus created by the first trench, removed to the far end of the bed so that it may fill in the final trench. I think the preferable method where space permits and where the bed is narrow is to excavate the whole of the top soil to the depth of 1 ft., placing this on the grass surround previously protected by sacks, and then spread a 2–4 in. layer of soaked peat to which has been added 6 oz. of coarse ground bones per

PLANNING AND PREPARATION

square yard on the exposed lower surface in the bed which is now 12 in. below ground level. This peat and bone should then be forked in as deeply as possible, mixing the added material thoroughly with this 'subsoil' as the lower strata is called. The top soil may then be shovelled back mixing with it more peat and bonemeal. The resulting bed in either case will be considerably higher than the surrounding soil, possibly 3-4 in. It is wise to allow the soil to settle before attempting to plant, although the bed will remain above the surrounding level. Consolidation will depend on weather conditions. The more rain the quicker the settlement but a minimum of four weeks should be allowed before planting.

When the bed is being prepared it is well to retain some of the best top soil and place it under cover to be used if the weather is wet when the bushes are planted (see page 31). Allow a cubic foot to each two plants. This earth, which should be damp but friable, never wet and sticky, may be placed about the roots of the bushes as they are planted and will assist in establishing them more quickly. So often at planting time the autumnal rains have made the soil too wet so that the earth turns over in sticky lumps which leave big air pockets and fail to make close contact with the roots. A little dry soil worked into the finer roots will allow air and encourage earlier growth, a lasting benefit to the plant.

This chapter has presupposed that the planting site is a new one. It may be that on changing houses one finds oneself in a tiny overcrowded garden heavily planted, and a jungle of weeds. Here time must be taken to restore order and fertility and also to take stock of what is there. There are 'knock-down weed killers' which will kill weeds by contact. They are no respecters of growths and cannot discern weeds from plants. If they are used the cultivated plants you wish to retain must be protected

THE ROOT

from the spray. Further, when the weeds have been killed they still stand as a sorry disgrace to the garden. Such weed killers may be used in a desperate emergency, but hand weeding to remove the whole weed is still the best method.

It may be that when such a clearance is made the site will be too small for a bed of roses but there is no reason why specimen or grouped bushes should not be grown among other plants—they are not snobbish and exclusive but they do need light, air and food, so they should not be grown near coarse overwhelming shrubs or near the pervading roots of coarse perennials. Choose the neighbours for your rose with discrimination and then an informal planting may be delightful and provide much pleasure. A list of specimen bush roses for 'lone' planting is given at the end of the book, see page 144.

2

Planting

After the bed has been prepared and has settled it may be marked out for planting the trees. The ideal way would be to dig a hole for each rose bush 9 in. deep and 15 in. square, having a slight mound 2 in. high in its centre. On this the plant would be placed with its roots spreading evenly in all directions. In actual procedure this is not practicable. In the first place, the roots do not radiate equally from the centre root. Further, a bed planted in this way would have the roses scattered unevenly, for an inch deviation of the bush while the bed was being planted would throw the plant out of the true row. The roots themselves may present a difficulty. When the plants arrive in the autumn the roots may well have been tightly bound until they are as deformed as the feet of a Chinese lady under the old régime. They should be loosened and spread out to restore their natural shape. If any of the roots have been damaged or are over long they should be shortened by cutting cleanly. It is unnecessary to have roots over long, and anything which will not slip into the hole prepared for the bush should be shortened. Roots should not be twisted to fit them into a confined space. Those which are left need room to produce fibre. Remembering the dry soil kept in reserve (see page 27), it is possible and advisable, where roots are on different levels, to allow them to remain in layers, thus a greater area of soil will contact the roots and more fibre will permeate all the soil.

THE ROOT

Twisted roots may be particularly noticeable in pre-packed rose trees because the package space is more limited and they may well remain longer in their confined space. Never buy a package rose where the bush including the root cannot be seen. While this subject is being discussed, roses which are purchased direct from a Garden Centre while they are in bloom or growing in containers should be noted. In such cases the roots should not be interfered with, but the ball of earth or planting material should be placed into the soil intact. Various mediums are used in these containers and some have little feeding value. It is essential to prepare the position for such roses and to add plenty of farmyard manure or peat with bonemeal. After a good watering the bushes should be allowed to settle in. Once new growth begins they should be fed as for dormant planted trees in their first spring. Some shelter may be needed for the first few days from hot sun or drying winds. However much care is given, it is not surprising if the battle for survival reduces the bush's energies so that it enters a period of semi-dormancy during which few blooms will appear. Much will depend on the previous treatment of the bushes while they were container grown, and good results are possible but can never be equal to those from dormant planted trees.

The simple and practical method of planting is to dig out a hole 9 in. deep and 12–15 in. square using one corner as the position for the bush, the roots of which would spread from the corner in a triangular space (see fig. 3). The soil from the first hole is saved and piled just outside the bed until the last bush is to be planted. The earth to fill the first hole is obtained from the second hole as this is being prepared for the second bush. After the roots have been covered with earth and well before the hole has been filled in, the soil should be trodden gently but firmly so that the roots contact the earth. After this

PLANTING

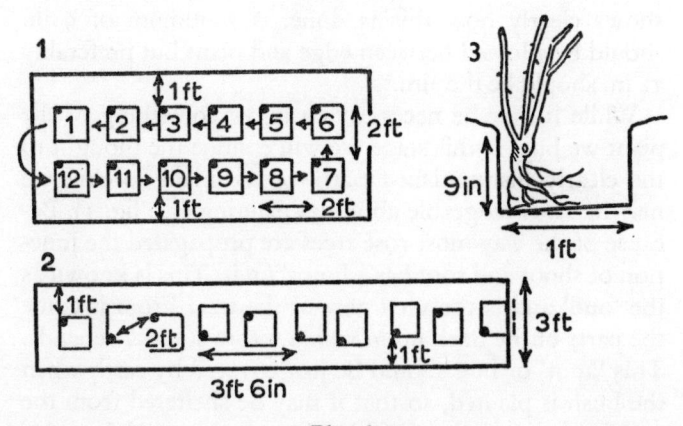

3. Planting

fill to within an inch of the top, tread again and leave the top inch without further treading. If the soil is wet during planting do not puddle the earth by heavy treading. If very dry, water thoroughly before the final inch of covering soil is added. Soil which has been saved and protected from the weather is the ideal material for working in among the roots if the soil in the bed is very wet. Small upright stakes or canes, one where each plant is to go, should be spaced over the whole bed before the work is started.

The ideal distance for planting rose trees varies with the type, but a general rule would be to allow about 2 ft. × 2ft. for each bush. It is better to plant two rows rather than one, and better still, to plant three rows wide as an impression of density and colour mass is more readily given. One does not have to plant with slavish precision at 2 ft. × 2 ft. The idea may be adapted. In a narrow bed 3 ft. wide a double row might be spaced with bushes at 3 ft. 6 in. apart in two rows 1 ft. apart, but with the bushes 'staggered'. This staggering is important and fig. 3 (2)

THE ROOT

shows clearly how this is done. A minimum of 9 in. should be allowed between edge and plant but preferably 12 in. should be the aim.

While it may be necessary to know something of the plant we buy, at this stage we will confine the thought to the clearly distinguished parts of the plant so that we may be knowledgeable about its planting (see fig. 1). Because of the way most rose trees are propagated the junction of shoot and root has a 'knot' on it. This is known as the 'bud' and is the vital part of the tree. From it come the parts of the bush upon which future success depends. This 'knot' or bud should be just covered by earth when the bush is planted, so that it may be sheltered from the worst rigours of wintry cold or summer heat and drought. An inch below the ground is the ideal but one must remember that the settling earth will recede so that when planting settlement must be allowed for. This means the actual planting should be done so that the junction of stem and root is at least 1½ in. below the ground at planting.

For general purposes nothing can beat planting during the dormant season. In such a time the plant will be able to recover from the very drastic treatment it received when its roots were cut and exposed to air. This exposure may be a dangerous condition if it is not controlled. During this period there is loss of moisture both from the root and stem, and the grower does his best to minimize the loss. In the first place the stems are shortened, in bush roses to 18 in., and in other types proportionately. This saves the immediate loss of moisture and reduces the danger from wind rock when the plant is exposed to high winds in the open garden. Secondly, the bushes when lifted are protected from exposure as far as possible. This happy state should be continued when the bushes are first received and the package opened, under cover. The roots

PLANTING

should never be exposed to drying wind as they are planted. They should be kept rolled in a wet sack and taken out from it and planted one at a time after the hole has been made for them. If they arrive in a dry condition, or if the soil is dry, they may well be plunged into a pail of water for two or three hours. In the unhappy event of their arrival being greatly delayed and their appearing in a shrivelled condition, more care is needed. A hole should be dug, deep and large enough to take up to eighteen roses. These should first be soaked by total immersion for up to twelve hours, and then be laid full length into their 'grave', and the soil filled in leaving a shallow depression (see fig. 4). This should then be filled with water and after-

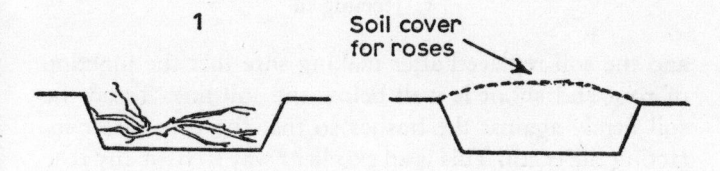

4. Resuscitating very dry plants (section)

wards the remaining soil heaped on. The bushes should be left some days, but a week should be the limit. On taking them out, if recovery is possible, they will be fully returned to normal. During the despatching season many thousands of orders have to be delivered in a limited time. Bushes may be sent away while weather conditions are good for planting. By the time they have arrived all may be altered. Either frost or heavy rain may prevent planting. Here is a second use for the heap of dry soil thoughtfully provided against such an emergency. The package may be undone, the roots released and unravelled, and the bundle inserted within the soil until the roots are well covered. If the soil has been under protection outside it may be covered again to preserve from frost or rain.

Where no such provision is possible a small area of soil should be kept frost free by covering with sacking, or even an old coat. Anything which will prevent frost penetrating. After opening the parcel, the roses should be 'heeled in'. This consists of digging a trench about 12 in. deep (see fig. 5). The roots may be placed in the trench

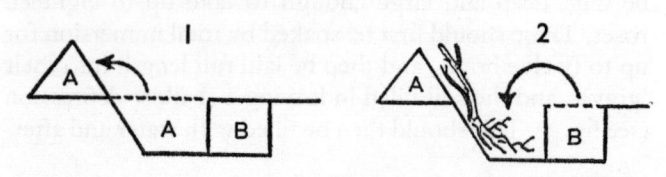

5. Heeling in

and the soil replaced after making sure that the junction of root and shoot is well below the soil line. Tread the soil firmly against the bushes so that the roots are contacting the earth. This is an excellent way to treat any rose bushes where planting is delayed. They will remain safely in such a position for many months.

One further emergency may be dealt with here. Any time during the dormant season when the soil is workable is a good time for planting roses. This is usually from mid-October until mid-March. At either extreme it is still possible to plant, provided the bushes are not dried out before they can re-root. This is a dangerous possibility especially in spring and may be prevented by pruning the bushes before planting, and then hilling up the plants so the tips alone are just visible (fig. 6). This prevents loss of moisture and as soon as growth begins the hills may be lowered carefully to avoid damage to shoots already growing under the soil coverage.

So far we have considered the making of new rose

PLANTING

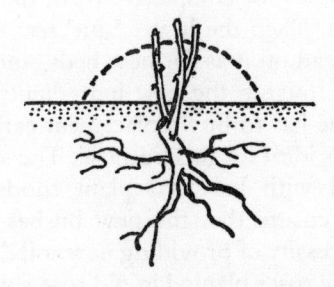

6. Hilling up

gardens and fresh beds on new soil. More often than not the new bushes are to replace those which have died or need replacing. Here the problem is one of soil. *Old soil in which rose trees have recently been growing is useless for new roses.* This is a fact. No actual reason can be given, although many guesses may be made. One thing is certain, if the new roses are to flourish they must have fresh earth. 'Fresh earth' in this case means soil in which roses have not been grown for at least three years. This may be obtained from other places in the garden, such as where perennials or vegetables have been grown. If one's choice is very limited the turf may be turned back and the soil under it exchanged for the old rose soil. The drawback in this last instance is the difficulty of allowing for settlement, in order to prevent the replaced soil under the lawn becoming bumpy owing to uneven settlement. In all cases the rose soil may be used by exchange, and other plants will flourish in it. If a single plant is to be introduced into an old rose bed, at least a cubic foot of earth should be removed so that the new bush may have this new soil around its roots. Where a whole bed is to be changed, at least 12 in. of fresh earth should be introduced after a similar depth has been removed. In this case it is better

THE ROOT

to clear the first foot completely from the whole bed in one operation. Then the lower 'spit' may have peat and bonemeal spread on it as for new beds, and this soil may be forked up, mixing the new ingredients well into the old soil. If one has to buy replacement earth, then 'John Innes No. 3' is ideal for this purpose. The soil is sterilized and prepared with balanced plant foods in sufficient quantities to ensure that the new bushes make a good start. This necessity of providing new soil does mean hard work, but new roses planted in old rose soil will languish rather than grow. Experiments are now being made which, if they are as successful as they promise to be, should revolutionize present methods, but the new materials will be costly and are dangerous in inexpert hands. Di-Trapex is such a material. It may be more generally used when the present experiments over large-scale areas have provided more experience.

This consideration of planting will be incomplete without some reference to staking. Standard rose trees (see fig. 15) and others need supports and these should be prepared well beforehand. Pergolas, lattice and stakes need

7. Watering a climber or rambler planted against a wall

treating for weather. 'Cuprinol' is harmless to the plant and is a most effective preservative. Not only should the portions below ground be painted or dipped; the portion at or near soil level is especially vulnerable. It is preferable to treat all the area exposed to weather. Stakes of wood for standards are usually 1 in. × 1 in. and they should be matured before use or the unseasoned wood may well bend and become useless. The hole for the plant should be opened and the stake driven into the harder subsoil before the roots are spread out. Where climbers and ramblers are planted near walls or other dry positions it is well to sink an empty 5-in. flower-pot level with the soil 18 in. away from the plant (see fig. 7). Watering should be done regularly through this flower-pot about once a fortnight until the plant is established.

While I have written much about the bush and its planting, the beginner will find that once the first and greatest hurdle has been passed successfully, the rest of the season's race may be run at an easy gallop.

3
Cultivation and Manuring

Once the rose bushes are safely planted there is little to be done immediately. That little may be very important, both with older and newly planted bushes. Both should be shortened by removing the heavy spreading growth at the top. A tall bush gives a big pull for a high wind when the soil is soft and as the bush blows to and fro a considerable hole will be worn in the soil where the plant enters the ground. This is a dangerous situation. The heavy rains may be succeeded by sharp frosts and the pool of water left in the hole will freeze and damage the bush just where it needs protection. Even if the bush, whatever its age, is shortened by removing half its growth, there may be some wind play. A watch should be kept throughout the winter and where the bush is loosened the soil should be trodden firm again. Wind damage may well occur where staking is employed for standard forms or where ties and pergola posts are concerned. A little timely care will save much hard work and even devastation at a later date.

As the weather improves with spring's advance the bushes will awaken. The major task, pruning, will be dealt with in a separate chapter. 'Tidying' the bed may be our next consideration once pruning is completed. It cannot be said too often, nor stressed too much, that the rose bush is a shallow rooted plant as far as its fibre is concerned. Beds should *never* be dug or forked over. During winter rains and snows the surface soil may be consoli-

CULTIVATION AND MANURING

dated and it is advisable to open the soil sufficiently to allow air to enter and for the wet surface to dry. This may be done by pricking lightly with a fork for the first 1½ in., or breaking the surface with a hoe when the weather improves. Care should be used at all times, for a hoe may inflict a nasty wound at the surface level of the rose branches which will lead to canker with its stem-rotting possibilities. Often a clump of annual grass will nestle at the foot of a bush. Remove it by hand, remembering that unless done with care this friendly act may be rewarded by a thorn if the finger and thumb are bare.

When the soil has been cultivated the feeding programme may begin. This is the best opportunity of the year for restoring fertility and adding plant food. It may be helpful to remember that feeding the soil has two important sides. One, often forgotten, is to improve the texture of the soil which is a living mass of organisms without which no life can exist. Vegetable matter as it decays produces humus and without this ingredient the soil is an inert mineral mass without life and unable to support life. That is why so much stress is laid on the addition of humus which may be in the form of farmyard manure, peat, seaweed or good compost. One's object should be to build up the fertility of the soil as well as to supply the plants' immediate need. This feeding may be done by artificial fertilizers with good results if the ingredients are well balanced, but any organic manure (i.e. of animal or plant origin) usually supplies some food as well. In this connection one must remember that peat has no food value. It acts as a sponge to absorb water and hold plant foods for the roots to find and in consequence is of very great mechanical worth.

This is a book for the beginner and my advice would be not to attempt to mix your own plant foods and never over-feed. This last occurrence is far too frequent. Newly planted bushes, if correctly fed when planted, should need no further help during the first growth period. For the others it is advisable to obtain a good compound rose manure, or if only a little is required, a good tomato manure will do equally well. For those interested, these foods should contain a low percentage nitrogen (5), a high phosphate (12) and potash (15) content. The dosage should never exceed the amount specified on the packet. An extra ounce per square yard is the equivalent of more than a hundredweight per acre. Generally speaking the total dose for the year should not exceed 4 oz. per square yard, 2 oz. of which should be given in early March and 2 oz. in mid-July. Never feed in the autumn with chemical (inorganic) fertilizers except for sulphate of potash, at the rate of 2 oz. per square yard, which is especially useful in early September after a wet summer. This dosage will help to harden the wood and tone up the plant for winter.

With organic manures the position is different. Usually these require considerable time before the plant can use them so that they may be hoed in lightly in late autumn. Among these are bonemeal, hoof and horn, and shoddy (dried blood is too rich in nitrogen to be recommended). Farmyard manure, well rotted and of good quality, i.e. with a high proportion of dung saturating the straw, is still the best feed. If possible its origin should be known as some types of weed-killing sprays used on the growing straw crop may still be lethal to plant life. Where good farmyard manure is obtainable it should be well rotted and then a 2-in. covering spread around the bush directly after pruning. This not only feeds the bush but helps to conserve the moisture. If this is considered too unsightly add a further ½ in. covering of broken peat to hide it in early May. Farmyard manure has the double advantage of supplying not only basic foods but trace elements, and as the straw decays, helpful bacteria and moisture-

CULTIVATION AND MANURING

absorbent material (humus) contribute to the general health of the plant.

Poultry manure if fresh contains too much nitrogen, but well rotted and mixed with peat it may be used with caution. An unfortunate by-product is often the increase of annual nettles, which are not checked by sprays.

More easily obtainable is mushroom manure. Personally, I am strongly against using this for two reasons. Too much lime may be added to the soil, and the enzymes produced in the growth of the mushroom spawn stop the straw from natural decay. The total effect on rose bushes is to weaken them and make them more prone to fall victim to disease.

The bed will benefit from a mulch. This is a protective layer, usually organic, which helps to retain moisture and eases the work of cultivation. The first application of artificial feed should be given before mulching and lightly hoed in. Peat is ideal for this purpose and should be first broken, thoroughly soaked and spread an inch thick over the whole bed.

This is the major task and given this treatment the root will now take care of itself.

One trouble which may happen must be considered, but to understand its importance something should be said about how rose bushes are produced. Some forty million rose trees are grown annually by nurserymen. To propagate this vast number successfully demands special methods. To obtain bushes of even growth and quality, the beauty and variety of the modern rose has to be wedded to a vigorous and hardy type such as the wild briar rose. The usual method is by 'budding'. To do this a small portion of the garden variety containing a piece of growing tissue within which is a dormant growth shoot (the budding eye) is removed from the parent plant. The wild stock is grown on in the nursery and when the sap is

THE ROOT

running strongly, the root bark is lifted, after a T-shaped incision has been made, and the budding eye is inserted beneath the outer bark and fastened firmly. Uniting with the stock, it becomes a dormant rose tree. The following spring, the top of the stock is cut away and the dormant 'budding eye' of the garden variety is forced into growth, producing a plant in the same year.

We have now succeeded in artificially making a new plant and the stock may not always take to its new top completely. Sometimes the stock may attempt to grow again. In this case a new shoot will be thrust up from the root. This is known as a 'sucker' and, unless removed com-

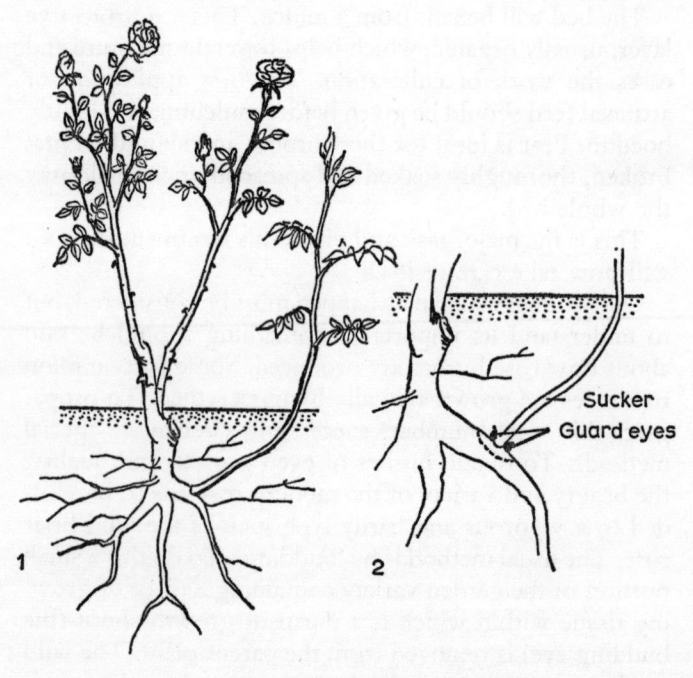

8. Suckering

CULTIVATION AND MANURING

pletely, will ultimately strangle the rose forced upon it. It is essential to realize that each 'sucker' has the potential of a new briar plant, and being lower than the rose has the first call on the full food supply from the root. These shoots should be left long enough for their nature to be certain and may then be removed by grasping them firmly and detaching from the root by a sharp upward jerk. Before this drastic attack begins the bush should be kept firm by pressing the foot against it to prevent the whole bush from being pulled out. Never cut the sucker. From every one which is cut will come three more. Where old bushes are throwing such shoots it may well pay to lift the whole bush, pull off the sucker and replace. Suckering is a natural hazard but it may be increased if the bed is cultivated too deeply and the roots become scratched. If the bush is damaged by frost or disease so that the energy of the root is not fully required for the top, the formation of a sucker diverts some of the waste strength (see fig. 8).

It is often difficult for the novice to distinguish a sucker. If in doubt wait until you are sure. Uusually it may be recognized by its paler green colour, its smaller leaves with more leaflets, its thinner growth which is more uniform along its whole length and its lack of flower at the top. If you are still in doubt, remove the soil carefully and trace the shoot to its origin. If it is a sucker it will be at a point below the shield of the bud.

Do not confuse the lush thick red shoots springing from the base of the bush with suckers for these will make the new branches of the rose bush.

By now the reader will understand why the root has been given prior place. It may not be as exciting or honoured as the flower, but no good results are possible without a sound root system, and a well-grown bush planted carefully will flourish for a minimum of ten years.

PART II
The Shoot

4
Pruning

Now that we have dealt with the root, hidden and unseen, we come to the superstructure of the plant, and because we can see it growing we need less reminding of its great importance.

With the shoot there will be three stages. The dormant time when little or no growth will be evident, the growing time when the leaf buds unfold, the leaves develop and the shoots mature with the final stage, which in most cases will be considered as the time of flowering, although in a few cases the ornamental fruits will be the climax for the bush. These periods may well overlap, and in some mild areas old leaves will hang on until the new growths push them off.

A healthy plant must be our first objective, and it is well to remember that the shoot may tell its own tale to those who are willing to observe. Weak, unhealthy wood, pale anaemic foliage, puny and weakly flowers must be considered as symptoms, and very often the cause of these troubles will be traceable to faulty feeding or poor root action.

Heavy feeding may weaken the young plant just as steak and onions might increase the troubles of someone with a weak digestion.

When we begin to consider the growth of the plant and its needs, we have to think of the framework of the plant and how to encourage the optimum of healthy wood and flower. Mere quantity is not the answer. Overcrowding of

THE SHOOT

the shoots can be as bad as a slum for producing disease. Light and air are essential for healthy plant growth.

This is the main reason for pruning, which may be defined as the removal or reduction of plant shoots to ensure the maximum of healthy growth in the best place.

If one is able to examine a wild briar it will be seen that each shoot has a period of growth, a period of flowering and fruiting and then a period of decline. If this were all, the bush would die out but this does not happen. When the branch has reached maturity and the crop of fruit has been carried, another young and vigorous growth springs from the base. This not only perpetuates the plant, it also hastens the death of the previous growth diminishing its food.

This is the key to pruning: firstly to encourage young and vigorous growth, secondly to remove ageing and weakly wood. An important factor is that by removing such wood much latent disease is removed and destroyed. There is another reason for pruning which can be very important and that is to fit a plant into its position.

I do not propose to give 'rule of thumb' instruction for pruning in this part of the chapter. Experience has taught me that if the reason for the treatment can be given then adaptation is easy. The interest and even delight in pruning is to be found in altering the rule to meet the emergency. The bush is living and therefore individual and unless the reason for the rule is clearly grasped our work is uncertain.

When one speaks of pruning to three or four leaf buds (see figs. 13 and 14) these instructions need not be carried out slavishly. It will pay the beginner to count these eyes for a time and once the idea of length of shoot and position of eye has been mastered an approximation will be all that is needed. It is the position of the top eye when left and the way in which it is cut which really matters.

PRUNING

The 'eye' the dormant leaf shoot which develops in the axil of the leaf may not be very prominent. Even if the shoot-to-be is not easily seen it is still there in the axil of the leaf stalk, and by cutting just above the leaf we are bound to cut just above the 'leaf bud' or 'eye'. It may show more as a scar than a rounded developing bud, but in counting the 'eyes' to leave, every dormant bud, each scar, should be counted, excluding only those which may be crowded round the base of a shoot. These dormant eyes will appear just like the one depicted in fig. 9. Such eyes do not appear on one side of the branch only. They occur at spaced intervals in a spiral fashion so that foliage and later shoots springing from the 'eyes' indicated by the foliage grow at different angles and levels of the shoot.

Another general thought. Correct pruning should always take the bed as a whole into consideration. It is unwise to leave a few very vigorous shoots high above the general level. Some degree of uniformity is advisable.

The first decision to be made will be how the plant carries its flowers. This will be seen under Chapter 7.

The next question generally asked is: 'If pruning is necessary, how do you know when and where and how to cut?'

As for when, I always advise spring pruning, as early as possible after the sap begins to rise. This is not hard to tell. The top leaves of a shoot grow first and when the tiny leaves begin to show growth, look at the eyes in the axils of the old leaves or where the old leaves have dropped. These tiny eyes will be seen swelling and shining. Such a time is between late February in the South and mid-April in the North or on high exposed positions. Some long-shooted varieties, such as climbers and ramblers, are better pruned and tied in before the autumn gales begin.

Where to cut? Observation shows that generally a rose

THE SHOOT

shoot when it begins to grow a second year will not throw more than three side shoots, all of which are close together and at the top of the growth. This means if the shoot is 24 in. long there will be 18 in. of straight shoot finishing at the tip with 6 in. of branching growth. Pruning ensures that the 24-in. shoot is reduced to 6 in. of growth, all of which is actively employed producing good flowering wood near the root—its food supply (see figs. 13 and 14). In the diagrams the 'eyes' on the branch are shown. Each of these may be a potential shoot. As light and air are essential the ideal is to encourage the top 'eye' to grow in an outward direction. This can be done by choosing as the top eye one that points in an outward direction.

The majority of bush type roses respond to such treatment and if new growth is pruned to three eyes the tree will grow taller at about the rate of 6 in. a year, producing more branches with each pruning. One point should be borne in mind. It is better to make sure that at least one new branch grows out from the base of the plant each year to provide for the necessary renewals of old wood. Prune at least one shoot on each bush very hard back (to one 'eye') each year after the first season.

Major pruning will vary with type, but if we carry in our minds a picture of what we want—plenty of strong new shoots with enough space to breathe and grow—we shall succeed. Treat all your first-year bush trees by hard pruning the first season, that is to three or four eyes—whichever gives a top bud facing outwards. Do not be afraid to cut and after the first time when growth begins and you are able to observe the result, this will give you confidence for the following year. Do not confuse the shortening of the bush as it leaves the nursery with the pruned bush. Always spring prune as instructed.

Another reason which may be given where older trees, especially shrub roses are concerned, is pruning for health.

This type of rose will flower for some years on its old wood. When growth weakens the whole branch should be removed. Such old wood may well carry disease spores through to the following year and so infect healthy new growth if it is left.

So far, we have been speaking as if the beginner were in a new garden. One of the major problems he may have to face is being confronted with old rose bushes in a mature garden. A lady who will discard an expensive hat at the end of a season without a sigh, will often lavish much time and money trying to resuscitate an old rose bush which should have been discarded for what it was —a liability. Provided the bushes are healthy they may be brought back to a good condition however rough and unsightly they may seem. Health is the point at issue. Old, weakly, diseased bushes are not only a liability themselves but may be a source of infection, especially to new bushes. It is a point to remember that newly planted bushes, like beginners at primary school, are far more liable to infection than old bushes which establish some form of resistance. 'If in doubt—out' should be the motto for old bushes. (On replacing a single old bush in a bed with a new one, see Chapter 2, page 35.)

Where the bush is old but vigorous its pruning presents a real problem. Yet the method is the same. Sometimes one seees a branch, perhaps an inch through, with 18 in. of bare shoot from which a young bush seems to be growing at its top (fig. 9). The answer is the same. Cut to three eyes, i.e. to 6 in. or so. But where is the eye? The leaf fell years before, but even so, on examination we shall see the scar left by the fallen leaf, and deeply embedded the tiny 'eye' just showing in the bark. With care and good cutting all the latent energy which has by-passed this dormant eye to feed the top growth, may be diverted and cause new branches to grow, making a new bush with

THE SHOOT

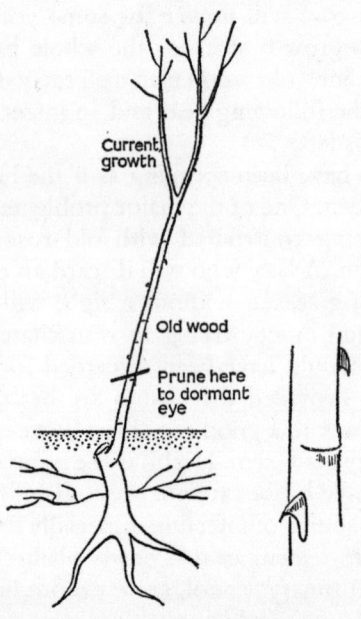

9. How to prune an old bush with vigorous growth at the top but a length of bare wood near the base. (*Right*) the scar from which the leaf fell, perhaps years before, above which, hidden in the bark, is the tiny dormant eye

balanced growth out of an unwieldy specimen. 'Careful cutting' was mentioned and it would be well to make a preliminary incision round the whole branch so that the weight of the detached growth as it is removed, might not tear the bark and destroy the bud on which so much depends. Probably the easier way to deal with such coarse growth is to saw off the top shoot and trim the stump cleanly above the eye. Where courage is lacking to take the risk it may be advisable to cut back half the old growths to the full extent on each bush and prune the remainder the following year.

PRUNING

The way to make the pruning cut is best seen by studying fig. 10. The cut should be clean, sloping away from

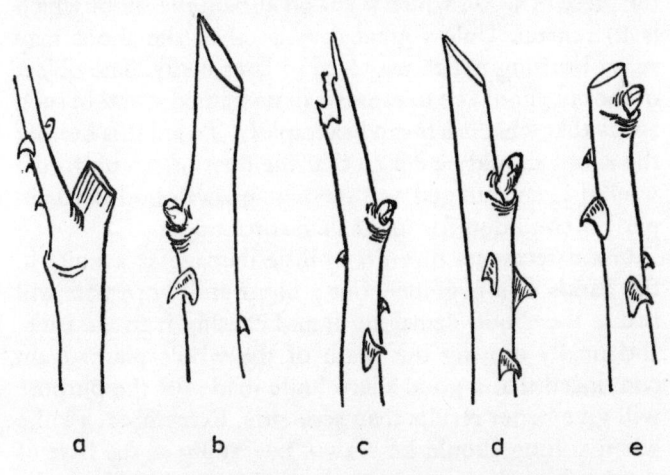

10. PRUNING CUTS: WRONG AND RIGHT

(a) The result of wrong pruning—the over-long snag has died back and this area of dead wood may allow entrance to fungi which will go on to attack the living wood
(b) Over-long snag above bud
(c) Damaged wood with over-long snag
(d) Cut made with wrong slope
(e) Correct clean cut

the 'eye', but sufficiently above the eye to prevent damage. The reason for the slope is to shed water and promote healing, as the sap rising to the eye will provide a 'callus' (protective growth) to heal the wound.

The cut in pruning should be considered as a surgical operation. That is, the cut should be clean and made under hygienic conditions. The cleanest cut can be made by a sharp knife with a slightly hooked blade so that the softer bark will yield as cleanly as the tougher wood.

THE SHOOT

Secateurs are probably more generally used, especially by beginners, but by their nature they exert pressure both on the piece of wood which is cut off and on the shoot which is to remain. Unless great care is taken the shoot may suffer bruising which may lead to later decay. The object of the cut should be to remove all unwanted wood in such a way that what is left can heal rapidly. To aid this healing the shoot should be cut so that the flow of sap up to the wound is encouraged and the first growth bud is left in perfect condition for immediate sprouting.

Good secateurs may do as little damage as a knife in the hands of a beginner, but a blunt and worn pair will bruise the shoot, damaging it and causing it to die back, and finally causing the death of the whole plant. I am convinced that a good sharp knife made for the purpose will give better results than secateurs. Remember, a knife when cutting should be drawn, beginning at the base of the blade and working to the point; it should not be pulled. If the shoot is drawn gently towards one as it is being cut it will yield more easily.

One of the greatest assets in pruning is a pair of good gloves. An old pair of soft leather is preferable as one needs a supple protection.

On balance it is better to burn the pruned shoots and so remove a source of infection from the garden. Composting such may be a dangerous procedure.

While not strictly termed 'pruning' one might again mention the shortening of the bushes to prevent 'wind rock'. Where top growth is heavy, and the plants exposed to wind, roots may be torn and frost penetration encouraged if topping is omitted. This is a simple procedure and may be achieved by shortening the growths during the late autumn by about a third, to keep the bushes compact during the winter.

'Summer pruning' is really cutting flowers and flower

heads intelligently. The foliage is essential to further healthy growth. If there is a choice, remove a central shoot rather than one affecting the framework of the plant. Do not remove long shoots from young bushes. When cutting off flower heads cut to the first plump rounded eye. A little observation will give sense to this description (see fig. 11).

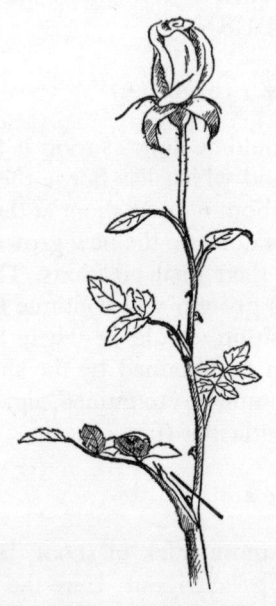

11. 'Summer Pruning'. Cut flowers (and dead flower heads) to the first plump rounded eye (in the axil of the first fully developed leaf)

A balanced bush well pruned will make for satisfactory growth and long life. The art of pruning can be learned in one way only, by practice. This does not mean that it is no use knowing the theory, which will make for intelligent understanding.

Much has been said about the cut. Study the diagrams and you will see why this should be clean and carefully planned. In the following paragraphs instructions will be short, but diagrams have been added where these can make the position clearer.

GROUP 1. RAMBLERS (for definition see p. 105) AND CLIMBERS

Ramblers, Type 1 (page 106)

This pruning should be done as soon as flowering ceases, when all the wood which has borne the crop should be cut out cleanly, about 6 in. of shoot at the base being left. As soon as this is done tie the new growths already made this season into their final positions. This work cannot be completed, as growth will continue for some weeks, but the final position should be where the maximum of light and air can be obtained by the shoots. Further, if possible, these should be fan trained, zigzagged or twisted out of the perpendicular (fig. 12).

Ramblers, Type 2

These are often more thick in shoot, larger in leaf and flower and have great vigour. Here the pruning may be later, in August or September, and all weakly or old wood should be cut out. The difficulty is that, having more vigour, a strong climbing shoot may develop some way up the stem. An example would be 7 ft. of new growth starting 5 ft. above the ground, growing out from a last year's cane. There is no reason why this surplus energy should not be used and left to develop a crop of flowers giving far greater range of growth than is possible in one year.

PRUNING

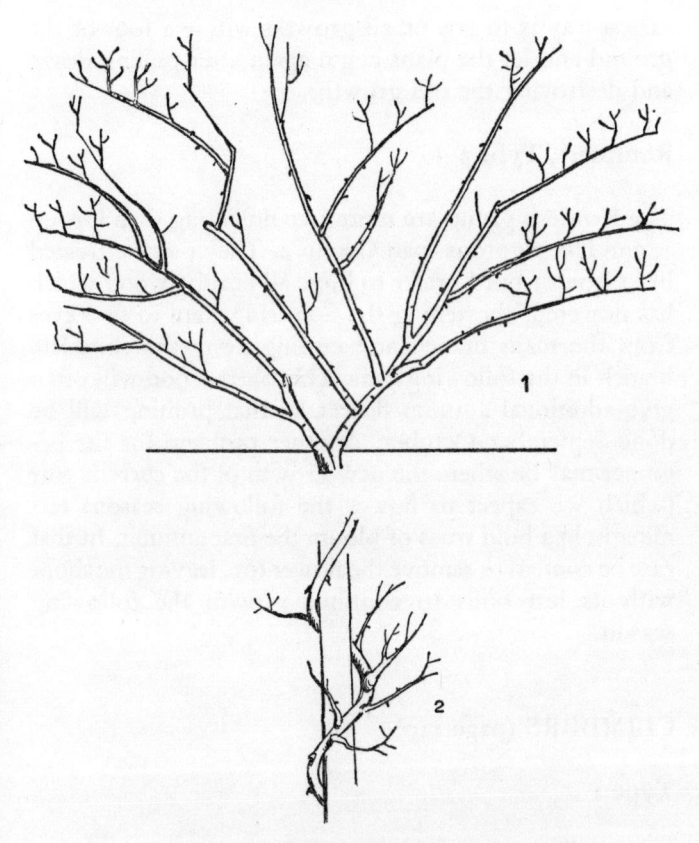

12. (1) Fan training of climbers and ramblers
    (2) Training round an upright post

If this type of pruning is adopted it is doubly important to cut at least one shoot hard back every year near ground level. Pruning such as this cannot be done where ramblers are inaccessible, for example, on the top of a shed or garage, until the competition becomes so fierce that many shoots are smothered and die. When this happens the easiest way is to saw off all growths within a foot of the ground and let the plant begin again after pulling down and destroying the old growths.

Ramblers, Type 3

The Kordesii group are more free flowering than Group 1, and less vigorous than Group 2. They may be treated like Group 1 but I prefer to leave all healthy wood which has flowered, shortening the flowering stem to two eyes from the main branch and cutting away the complete branch in the following year. This older wood will often give additional autumn flower so that pruning will be done September–October. Another problem for the beginner may be where the new growth of the current year (which we expect to flower the following season) terminates in a bold truss of bloom the first autumn. In that case be content to remove the flower top, leaving the shoot with its leaf buds to continue growth the following season.

CLIMBERS (page 110)

Type 1

'Sports' of bushes. When planting, these should not be hard pruned. It is wise for them to be shortened as the torn root system cannot produce enough food and moisture to maintain a large area of wood. These shorter 18–24-in. growths should be trained horizontally to encourage new and vigorous canes to grow from the bud.

Pruning the second year is negligible. Soft tip-growths should be cut off when tying in before the winter gales and that is all. The following year these shoots will flower. If there is room for new shoots and old growths as well, shorten back the flowering shoots on the old wood leaving inch-long spurs near the main branch. This system may be carried out for a further year if there is room for the new wood. If not, always tie in a new shoot and remove an old one where there is competition for the same space. Remember, a climbing rose needs three years to come to its full area of flowering. And what a flowering! A good specimen can give 300 blooms in one season.

Type 2. Perpetual

When one comes to perpetual climbers there is a great variety in growth. Some will be vigorous and may be treated as Type 1, but there are others which are like lanky bush roses. They flower on a tall terminal (end of shoot), then grow again just below where they flowered and then flower again on the second terminal. This they may continue to do, going up to 7 or 8 ft. if given time. All that should be done is to train them horizontally and cut off their flower-heads. The second year such shoots will grow and flower from the sides of the growth gradually building up a considerable bush which will give many flowers.

It will soon appear that there are some varieties that will grow vigorously under any conditions, and these we must shorten and thin vigorously, while there are others which must be encouraged even cajoled into making sufficient coverage for their purpose. In my suggested list the Types and Groups to which these roses belong will be given. This may mean that some border-line cases listed as climbers or ramblers will have their order reversed if the type of pruning necessary belongs to a different section.

GROUP 2. OLD-FASHIONED AND SHRUB ROSES, SPECIES, ETC. (see page 115)

It is quite impossible to give rule-of-thumb method for all members of these varied types. The same rules apply as for all roses and probably the most important point to remember is that one can do more harm by over rather than under pruning.

We should have in our mind's eye the objective of a shapely shrub. Cutting will be necessary only if the wood becomes weak and sickly when it should be removed completely. Some shoots must be taken away to protect the bush. A loose arching branch whipping about in a gale may not only reduce itself to shreds but may at the same time spoil other growths and by breaking away dormant eyes from these shoots reduce the flowering possibilities for the next year. Swaying shoots should be shortened enough to save damage to themselves and other growths.

This simple rule may be carried out for both tall and short types. If on observation a variety flowers on old and young wood then leave as much as possible. The overall picture is of a shrub with a great mass of flower. Quality of bloom is of little importance therefore thinning and reducing competitive shoots is unnecessary. But remember the usual rule should always apply, cut one shoot hard to gain new growths from the base of the tree, although doing this every other year may be enough.

GROUP 3. POLYANTHA AND FLORIBUNDA ROSES (see page 120)

The first year prune hard to two or three eyes, choosing an outer eye for preference. It is essential to get the bush

PRUNING

to send out shoots from ground level if it is to be permanently healthy. If all goes well such growths from the base will be produced for autumn flowering. *Year two* requires little cutting as most of the wood will be one

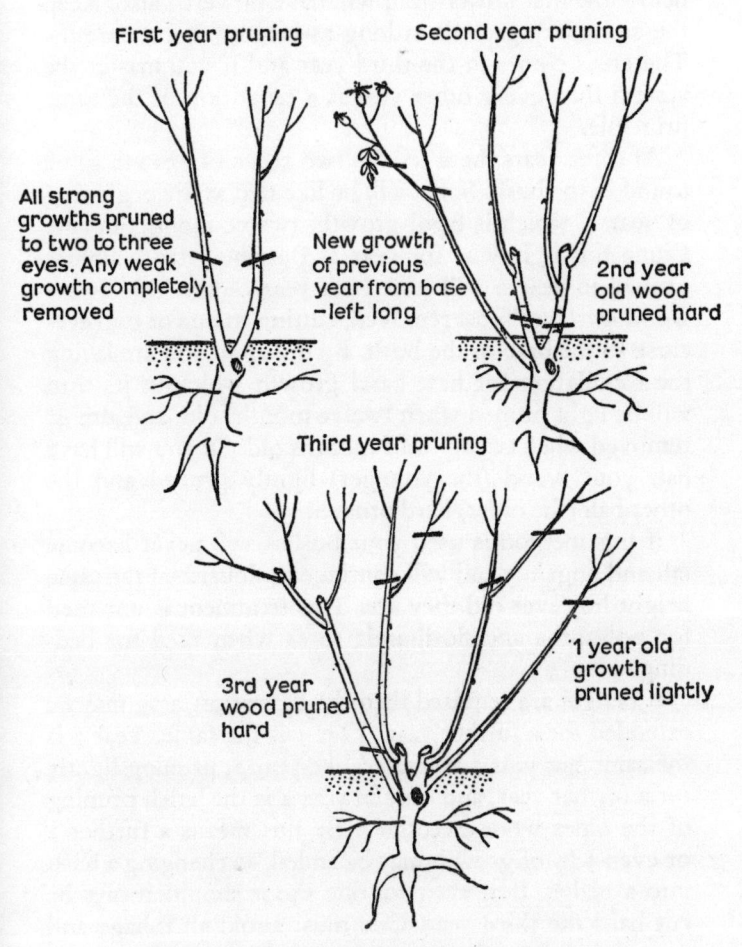

First year pruning

All strong growths pruned to two to three eyes. Any weak growth completely removed

Second year pruning

New growth of previous year from base – left long

2nd year old wood pruned hard

Third year pruning

3rd year wood pruned hard

1 year old growth pruned lightly

13. Pruning polyantha and floribunda roses

year old. All that needs to be done is to remove any thin growths, take off the flowering heads if they have been left on by mistake, and tip back to the first healthy 'eye'. Sometimes the secondary growth springing from just below the first flower-head will have flowered also. Keep the secondary growth as long as healthy wood permits. The crisis comes in the third year and if you master the system then every other year is a repetition of the same principle.

At three years there will be two types of growth to be found in the bush. Some will be like that at the beginning of year 2, which is basal growth, twelve months in age. Prune this lightly as for year 2. But the growth lightly pruned in year 2 will now be a year older. This 2-year wood *must* be almost removed, cutting to one or two eyes close to the base of the bush. By doing so you are laying the foundation for new basal growth which in its turn will be light pruned when twelve months old, and almost removed when twenty-four months old. So you will have half your wood (the younger) lightly pruned and the other half (the older) hard pruned.

If this method is used your bushes will never become tall and ungainly and will continue to flourish at the same height however old they are. This treatment is unvaried for polyantha and floribunda roses when used for bedding.

If hedges are required then the lighter pruning may be extended for a further year. Year 1 is the same. Year 2 is the same but year 3 is treated like year 2, pruning lightly for a further year, and only in year 4 is the harsh pruning of the older wood necessary. By this means a further 2 or even 3 ft. of growth may be added, so changing a bush into a hedge. But, even so, one shoot should always be cut hard the third year. One must avoid all foliage and growth being confined to the upper branches.

PRUNING

GROUP 4. BUSH ROSES (H.T.) (see fig. 14 and page 131)

The pruning of H.T.s is probably as simple as any.

Year 1. Prune to three or four eyes, choosing a bud which points outward as building up a cup-shaped bush

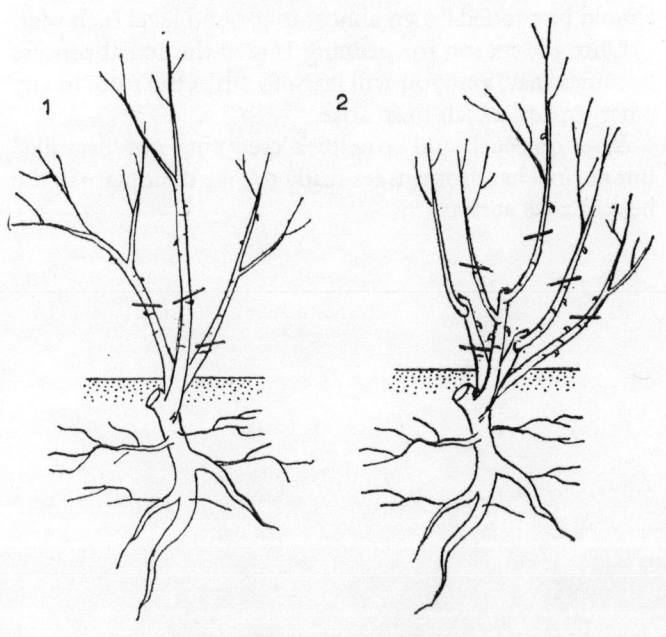

14. Pruning H.T. roses
(1) Year 1   (2) Year 2

with plenty of air room in the centre and with the branches as far as possible equidistant from each other, so that when the new growth comes it will have enough room. Dormant shoots at 3 in. apart may seem well spaced, but try to envisage each of those shoots with three growths

THE SHOOT

and imagine the ensuing chaos. If in pruning you have left too much wood the ill effect may be mitigated by rubbing away a few of the worst positioned growths when they are 1 or 2 in. long in April and May.

Year 2. Prune the new growths of the previous year to three or four eyes above where they started.

Year 3 will be the same but remember at least one shoot should be pruned down almost to ground level each year.

Once the reason for pruning is seen the actual process becomes easy, and you will learn to adapt the rules to any emergencies which may arise.

Your object should be neither 'crew cuts' nor 'beatniks' but normal handsome trees ready to take their place in the best of rose society.

Black Spot

Rust

Mildew

Aphides

Larvae of leaf rolling sawfly

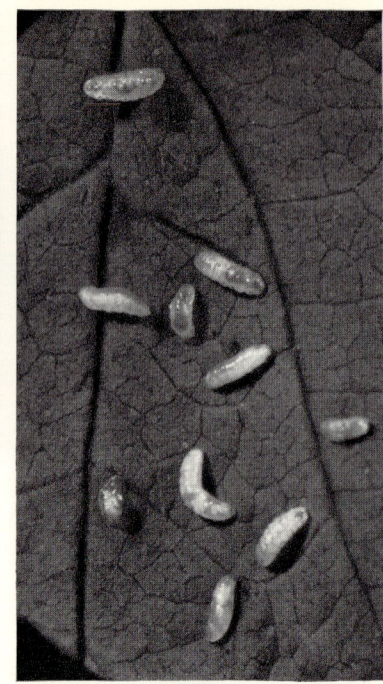

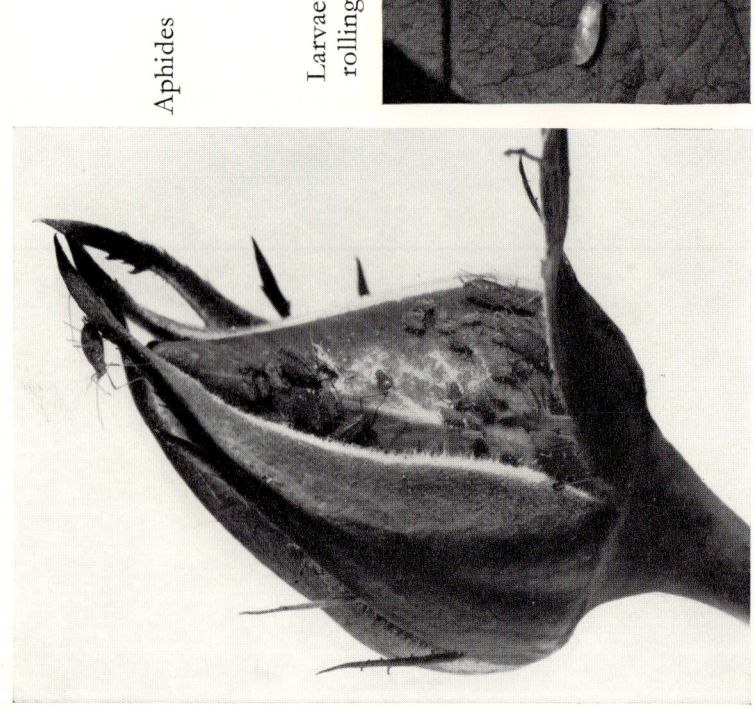

5
After-care: Pests and Diseases

There are a few rules on the use of sprays which should be written on the hearts of all gardeners. Firstly 'never spray unless you have reason to do so'. This does not mean no preventative spraying should be carried out but there should have been disease the previous year to warrant early spraying. Young leaves as they unfold are soft and easily damaged, and any sprays for disease should be started at half the advised strength. After that keep closely to the directions, especially as to strength. Apply the spray when the sun is not shining and avoid cold windy periods. The ideal time is in the evening when the sun has lost its power. Disease sprays are usually preventative. If the forecast is for rain get the spray on before it begins. The idea is to provide a complete preventative coating on the leaf surface so that disease spores cannot germinate. This gives an idea of frequency with which spraying is needed. A long dry spell may make spraying less necessary. A wet period will demand frequent spraying. Usually under normal weather conditions once a fortnight is as often as one needs to spray.

To take avoiding action is the golden rule for dealing with all disease, and as a precaution it is wise to spray all bushes with copper sulphate (1 oz. to a gallon of water) while the bushes are quite dormant, usually immediately after pruning. This should be regarded as routine treatment on all bushes and climbers. Indeed, every rose, even the species, should have its quota. It is wise to remember that copper sulphate at this strength can burn green plants, so that growths of other plants near the bushes should be protected during this initial spraying.

Treat all sprays with great respect. Many are poisonous and some are lethal. It is the plant you are spraying, not yourself! You will be wise to protect your hands with rubber gloves. The sprays mentioned during this chapter have been recommended by the Ministry as suitable for the purposes for which they are advocated.

Usually it is better to have a sprayer where the pressure can be raised before the application begins. There are many light spraying machines which can either be suspended from the shoulder or, where the area is small, stood on the ground, thus leaving both hands free.

Another point worth remembering is that complete coverage is essential. Both upper and lower sides of the leaf need the spray as well as shoots. This is much more easily done where the nozzle has a bent joint at the end of the lance. Always buy a better sprayer than you think you can afford. A good machine will ease the work and encourage you to use it regularly.

Mixing sprays should be done with great caution. The directions on each spray will tell you what other sprays may be used with it. Even so, it is better to keep disease sprays separate for best results. Black Spot needs a different interval of time between one spray and the next compared with Mildew. The latter needs more frequent spraying.

Over-spraying is a common fault and at the moment more harm is done by too much rather than too little. A fine mist which covers the leaf is the ideal, heavy applications leading to the drops running together and dripping may cause burning and defeats the object of complete and uniform coverage.

One's whole object should be to produce healthy vigorous plants which will stand up to adverse conditions and throw off disease. Few rose trees are immune from common diseases but many are more resistant than others. The best growth is vigorous but sturdy. Soft, lush wood must be avoided. This is not always possible, for warm moist conditions promote soft growth and also provide the ideal environment for disease.

Manures which promote soft and rapid growth contain a high percentage of nitrogen. Balance is essential and sulphate of potash helps to promote the right type of hardy growth.

'BLACK SPOT'

'Black Spot' is the commonest disease from which roses suffer, and there are many strains of the disease, some more adaptable and virulent than others. The signs are purplish-black roughly circular blotches with ragged edges which finally merge and kill the leaf, which then drops. Bad attacks are rapid and can defoliate a bush in the autumn. This is a disfiguring but not killing disease, although its weakening effect is obvious, and plants so attacked cannot stand cold conditions. Once the black spots shows on a leaf, it is too late for that leaf to be cured by spraying, but unaffected leaves if sprayed may be kept clean and continue their functions.

While Black Spot is common to every district, its ravages are kept in check in all industrial areas, and this protection may extend some miles farther when the prevailing wind carries the polluted atmosphere, although with the smokeless zones some areas formerly free are now getting disease. The same is true of 'Rust' which is more prevalent in the wetter and warmer areas of Britain but of little consequence in cities.

'Black Spot' sprays

At the moment the swing is in favour of MANEB. The reason for this is simple as it has a twofold reaction both on 'Black Spot' and 'Rust'. If the plants have had a bad attack the previous year begin with half strength in early May, otherwise June or even July may be early enough but always continue with regular applications once started. If you are going on holiday spray just before you leave. Bushes can be defoliated very rapidly by Black Spot in September.

For Black Spot only, Captan (Orthocide) is effective and I think leaves less visible residue on the foliage. Normally the interval between both these sprays is a fortnight.

'RUST'

'Rust' is a more dangerous disease and is particularly common in the warmer and wetter areas such as the south-west of England. While some sprays may be helpful it is better to sacrifice the odd plant and burn immediately when the first signs appear. 'Rust' can be killing. The leaves attacked lose their healthy appearance and grow dry and brittle. The spores appear on the under side of the leaf as a bright rust brown, from which the disease gets its name. Later these spores go black. The leaves fall and where the attack has started early the plant dies. It is a noteworthy fact that this disease thrives on moist, warm, pure air, and so is more prevalent in the south-west of England. MANEB is one of the few safe sprays to use against this trouble. Normally the timing may be as for Black Spot.

AFTER-CARE: PESTS AND DISEASES

'MILDEW'

One of the more disfiguring diseases. Only the form which affects outside roses need concern us here. The young growths become disfigured and twisted and are covered, both leaf and shoot, by a powdery white dust like a sprinkling of flour. Mildew is common and promoted by soft growth, lack of air and sudden variations of temperature. While a nuisance and unsightly, because it is more common in autumn the affected wood need not do any permanent damage for it will be removed later during routine pruning. It is not easy to control for the best sprays are very soluble and constant application is necessary. Every ten days is normal but after a heavy rain a further application is advisable. Such sprays should be kept away from paintwork. Here is another instance where the right feeding will produce resistant growth. 'Epsom Salt' provides magnesium which has proved helpful as an addition to the usual foods. This may be applied (1 oz. per sq. yard) or as 'Keserite' (2 oz. to the square yard) once a year in the spring.

For Mildew Karathane (Dinocap) is probably the best control but being highly soluble must be used frequently. It can be irritating to the skin, eyes and nose and is dangerous to fish. For greater effect it is probably better not to mix with other sprays. Where a few roses only are concerned then a dust with green sulphur may well be as effective.

These three diseases are the major troubles to be faced and quite enough for any beginner to start with!

PESTS

Pests are natural to all plant life. They need to feed just

as we do! It is a battle which should be won in the first engagement, even if skirmishes and 'mopping up' operations continue throughout the season. There are two types of 'livestock' to be dealt with—those which live by sucking the sap (the plant's life blood) and those which eat the leaf. The first are debilitating, weakening the plant's health overtly. The second are disfiguring because they destroy leafage and flower and so indirectly diminish the food supply of the plant. Excellent preventative results may be obtained by spraying with a fruit tree winter wash, D.N.O.C., at half strength during a mild spell in February but not later. This will kill off many eggs of pests, so decreasing later damage.

The commonest and most prolific pests are the 'Aphides', 'Greenfly' in their best-known form, although they may appear as amber, reddish or black variations. Their main strength lies in the rapidity with which they breed, and constant vigilance is well repaid. The line of attack must be to spray as soon as seen, not to wait for a build-up, and to spray twice with a three-day interval between to make sure that any stragglers are cut off. After this spray as necessity arises. Aphides migrate so that clean bushes can be re-infected very quickly.

A type of spray giving excellent results but needing care in application is Rogor. This is known as a systemic spray and is partly absorbed by the plant so that insects piercing the stem to suck out sap (like greenfly) or caterpillars feeding on the leaf are poisoned as they feed.

There are many other sprays to kill off greenfly. Malathion is probably one of the best for all sucking insects. It is harmful to bees and fish. Combined with D.D.T. it is even more effective and lasting but it is harmful to livestock as well as bees and fish. It is an organo-phosphorous compound and should not be used by allergic subjects.

Natural predators such as sparrows and ladybirds will

AFTER-CARE: PESTS AND DISEASES

keep small numbers within bounds and should be welcomed.

Probably the most damaging enemies after greenfly are the many forms of caterpillars and larvae which feed voraciously on the rose leaf. Generally speaking the finger and thumb method, crushing the specimens when seen, is sufficient. This does call for observation which adds to interest. Many of the leaf-feeding caterpillars make their meal at dusk, and the evening is the best time to observe them. Another type, more maggot than caterpillar, draws the leaf together and in this protected cell continues its work. Pressing the leaf on both sides is enough to crush this pest. More difficult to trace, and usually demanding a spray is the tiny grub which nips out the growing shoot in its very early stages, leaving a 'blind' shoot, i.e. one which has no flower bud at its end.

Mention should also be made of two types of a family which gives much trouble. These are the 'sawflies'. The leaf-rolling sawfly leaves a characteristic trail of trouble behind it. The fly, rather like a flying ant or elegant form of house fly, about a third of an inch long, haunts airless, still parts of the garden. Its eggs are laid in May and June on the outer edge of the leaf which immediately begins to curl up lengthwise. The larva when hatched continues to feed on the leaf within its self-made protection. Once full fed the larva drops into the soil and pupates to await the spring and another cycle. The damaged leaf turns yellow and drops. By reason of the colour of the leaf at this stage the trouble may be confused with chlorosis, a sign of iron deficiency. If this trouble is neglected there can be a rapid build-up in a few years. Sprays against sawflies should be applied in early and mid-May and again in June. The best is Malathion alone or Derris and D.D.T. together. Picking the leaf and burning it when it is rolled but still young and green may prevent a carry-over of many larvae. The second deterrent is to let in more light and air. A garden often becomes overgrown and airless when small shrubs make big trees. For this reason keep the rose area as clear of large trees and shrubs as possible.

The second, a very troublesome form of sawfly, is the rose slug worm. In this case the damage is caused by the larvae eating off the underside green layer of the leaf to leave a silvery skeleton. This can be very unsightly. The slug worm is just over a third of an inch long, nearly transparent. It feeds on the underside of the leaf during the day, but after a shower in dull weather, or in the evening, it may be seen on the upper surface of the leaf. Spraying is the only solution and should be carried out as soon as the first signs appear. The spray is the same as for the leaf roller but may have to be continued while damage appears. A second crop of larvae may extend into July and August if a first spraying has been neglected.

'Cuckoo-spit', the white froth substance found in the axil of the leaf is traceable to the 'Froghopper', a yellow creature which seeks protection in this froth while it pierces the shoot and sucks out the plant sap. Spraying with Rogor or hand-picking is the answer.

The leaf-cutting bee presents a problem that should be dealt with when the damage first becomes apparent. The rose leaves have small semicircular portions cut from them with mathematical precision. The bee has cut these leaf portions for nest making and its home, usually in an old wall, may not be easy to trace. With patience this can be done in the evening by tracking them down as they fly homeward and following up with D.D.T. spray.

So we come to the end of the more common diseases and pests of the rose. Their number should not deter us, for with care one may expect the minimum of trouble. The old saying 'Forewarned is forearmed' is undoubtedly true.

AFTER-CARE: PESTS AND DISEASES

It pays to visit and inspect your bushes with great care the week before you take your annual holiday. A preventative spray at this time may give a future clean bill of health by preventing a build-up while you are away.

6

Afterthoughts: Training, Staking and Tying; Hedges

Of the many types of rose trees grown for different purposes, those used to cover are generally considered as ramblers and climbers (see pages 105–114).

It should be understood that most vigorous bushes growing 5–6 feet may be used to cover walls.

The whole success of this type really depends upon the method of training. A simple illustration within most people's experience emphasizes this fact. At some time we have seen a rose climbing up the wall of a house. The older shoots as they have gone up vertically have neither branch nor flower, and yet as soon as a shoot has been pulled down horizontally below a window the whole branch has been full of side growths and blossom.

This is the key to the successful flowering of ramblers and climbers. Check the growth by bending out of the vertical. The ideal method is to fan train (see page 57), but this is only possible where a clear wall is to be covered. The method may be adapted to suit the situation. If these climbers have a restricted position they may be zigzagged, or if on a post they might be twisted round. All these methods are equally successful (see fig. 12).

Sometimes one inherits an old climbing rose, the main shoot or shoots of which are thick, coarse and leafless for the first length of many feet. Can new growth be encouraged under such conditions? The same principle is used.

TRAINING, STAKING AND TYING; HEDGES

When the top of the tree is growing freely (usually May–June) the whole should be untied and the tree allowed to lie prostrate on the ground. Usually, within ten days or so, the dormant 'eyes' at the base of the tree begin to break into growth. When this action has begun the shoot usually extends rapidly and the tree may be tied back into position, taking care to train the new shoots out of the vertical. When these are established the old wood may be removed.

One should remember that climbers can be very brittle and their growths should be bent with great care otherwise they may snap, and in breaking tear an additional strip of bark from the lower part of the branch, wasting a very considerable length of flowering potential.

Tying is so interwoven with training that this important subject should be dealt with now. The materials to be used are worth consideration. I prefer semi-permanent to permanent fastenings. Usually the tie should last twelve months but not longer. Shoots thicken greatly, and wire, whether covered or not, will bite into the living wood and cause the branch to snap at that point. A softer material is called for. This may be string of sufficient thickness to spread its grip so that the tissues in immediate contact are unbruised. This should have been treated with a preservative. Shoots grow very rapidly. I have known an 'American Piller' rambler to grow $4\frac{1}{2}$ in. in twenty-four hours. Because of this it pays to keep some tying material fastened near the support ready for immediate use. Always tie the shoot on to the support so that the growth is exposed to sun and air. Not only is this better for health but it is essential for accessibility. The whole object of the exercise is to have the plant fastened on to its support, not interwoven with it, so that when the time for pruning comes all the growths can be rapidly detached. The plant will then lie out on the grass or path.

THE SHOOT

The necessary removal of the unneeded shoots can be done quickly, easily and accurately. The shoots are then retied with the minimum of labour and discomfort. Trying to prune in position, piecemeal, is a painful business, and as the shoot is drawn away from its neighbour it may well scratch out the 'eyes' of the shoot which is left as well as inflict painful wounds on the operator.

If the suggested method is used with care the result is not only highly satisfactory in its effect but it proclaims to the passer-by that the work has been carried out effectively and intelligently.

A problem which may need solving is the distance to leave between growths. When the shoots are bare in the winter they may appear a long way apart, but one has to remember that side growths will be 15 in. or more and so they will more than cover the intervening space. Allowing for the flowers one should aim at a minimum distance of 15 and a maximum of 20 in. between branches when these are tied in.

Generally speaking one will find the ramblers have thinner and more pliant shoots than the climbers. The ramblers (see lists, page 105) flower on their twelve-month-old wood (July growth to July) and as soon as the flowers have finished they may be removed and the new growths tied in. This may be done from August onwards.

The climbers will flower not only on the wood like the ramblers but also on the side growths and even for a further year. These older shoots will not give such quality blooms but they give a larger quantity of smaller flowers spread over a longer period. The autumn flowering of a climber depends in part on keeping this older wood and experience will show that the less vigorous climbers (those growing up to about 8 ft.) give more autumn flower than the vigorous kinds.

There are other forms of training which should be

TRAINING, STAKING AND TYING; HEDGES

mentioned but the method is the same. Some steep banks may be covered by ramblers planted at the base and then trained up the bank. Instead of tying into position these should be pegged down where they are to grow. Bent wire pegs or stakes made of small notched branches which have been pointed may be used.

One of the types the training of which causes much heart searching is the weeping rambler. This is a specialist

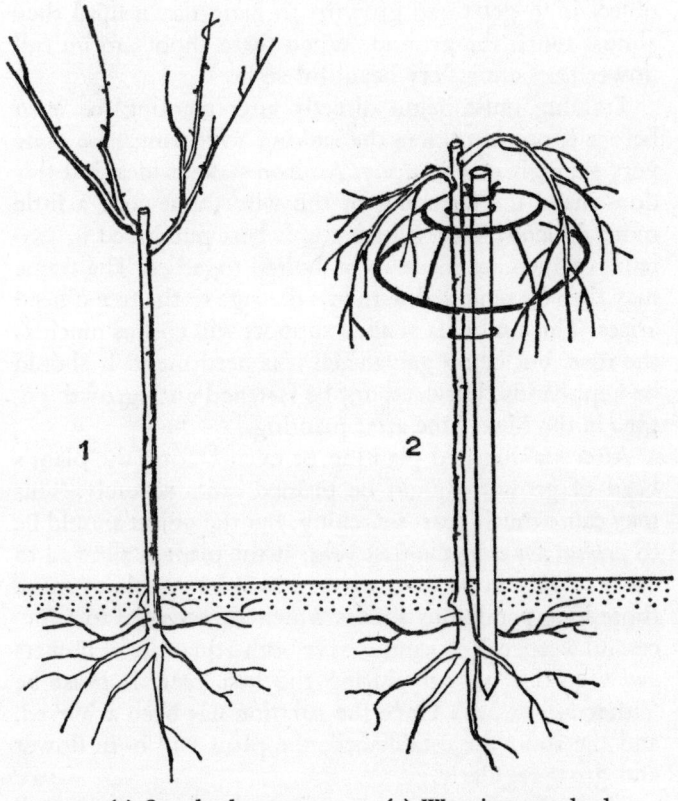

15. (1) Standard rose tree   (2) Weeping standard

THE SHOOT

type of standard tree (see fig. 15). If one can grow this type successfully it may be a focal point in the garden, but it must be treated with the care it demands. Unless one is prepared to spend time and money on growing it really well it is best left alone.

Weeping standards consist of a few specially suitable ramblers which are budded on tall (4½–5 ft.) growths. The idea is to encourage long pendulous shoots equally spaced around a circular support to which they are fastened. The object is to get these growths to hang down until they almost touch the ground. When these shoots are in full flower they are a very beautiful sight.

Training must begin directly after planting, or even before if one considers the staking which must be done very strongly and securely. An iron stake is ideal but this does make the fastening of the wire framework a little more difficult. This wire frame is best purchased in two halves which are made to be bolted together. The frame may then be removed with less damage to the tree if need arises. This umbrella shaped support will cost as much as the rose, but being galvanized it is permanent. It should be kept handy, but need not be fastened until growth begins in the May–June after planting.

After staking and planting or even before, the plant's head of growth should be pruned quite severely. This may cause much heart searching, but the object should be to *prevent flowering* the first year. If the plant is allowed to flower freely in its first season it will be unable to make those long pendulous shoots which are essential to a successful weeper. You cannot have both a quantity of flowers *and* vigorous growth during the first year. It must be 'either . . . or . . .'. Once the rotation has been achieved, and the roots are established, the plant will both flower and grow regularly.

The only way during the first spring is to shorten all

major growths to 6 in. and cut away completely any wispy growths. This will make a short head instead of a 'crown of glory', but the future should be assured.

After fastening the hoop one must wait for the shoots to grow and as they lengthen they should be led over the top of the hoop and tied down on to its outer circular wires at spaced intervals. It is better to use raffia so that those ties can be replaced as more growth takes place. One must not expect to achieve full growth in the first year, but when a start has been made the same idea must be repeated year after year. Tie in the new growths from the centre of the head and remove the old shoots immediately they have flowered. This sounds complicated but in practice the method will gain in clarity as we continue.

Much time has been spent on this form of training, but once mastered many years of striking beauty may be anticipated. Make sure all attachments are secure. If an iron stake is not used check the wooden stake especially before winter and during the summer at flowering time.

Tying is a most important item. If it is omitted or carried out carelessly much irreparable damage may be done. One does not realize how heavy a plant saturated with much rain and buffeted by gale may be. More damage is done by insecure tying or poor staking in the summer than in winter. Tying material is very important. It needs to be soft and easily tied, and for this reason wire is out. Sisal or fillis should be weather-proofed and although tarred string is good it is messy to use. For standard roses there are special ties with rubber cushions and material for fastening. These are expensive but last a long while, and because they stretch, do not cut into the swelling stem. The matter of 'cushioning' a permanent stem is important and where webbing band or string is used it is as well to pass the material round the stake first, so making a barrier between stake and tree, thus avoiding chafing.

Stakes should be well made. A stick has too short a life. For standard roses the stake needs to be 5 ft. long and 1 in. × 1 in., pointed and seasoned. This should be driven firmly into the sub-soil when the planting hole has been excavated. The first tie should be of a temporary character as settlement will take place and the first tie will need altering in a month or so. It is most important that all stakes and woodwork should be treated with cuprinol. This greatly lengthens the life of the wood and increases its reliability and the safety of the supported bush.

What has been said about stakes applies just as forcibly to pergolas (wooden frameworks to support climbers), posts and trellis. Make these of strong lasting materials. The best woods are sweet chestnut or oak. So often the rotting takes place between air and soil, and if the post can be inserted in a concrete footing which rises a foot above the soil these posts should outlast the rose. Larch poles look 'arty' but have a short life, and, by providing hiding-places for pests and diseases beneath their loose bark, are not to be recommended.

A trellis, to be effective, should be specially made with 7-in. squares. It should be well 'cuprinolled' on back and front and fastened to the wall on 3-in. wood blocks so that the air can circulate freely between wall and plant. This extra care reduces the likelihood of Mildew, and also allows the wall to dry. If you are having a house built, arrange for the builder to place vine eyes in the wall as building proceeds.

A word about surrounds to a garden should be considered. Walls make the ideal but usually these are prohibitive in cost. Generally speaking a plastic netting hedge may be used (black will be less obvious than green) or wattle (which treated and kept off the soil is fairly lasting) or woven fencings. On no account should corrugated iron be used. This becomes extremely hot and then

Maigold (Perpetual Rambler)

Albertine Rambler

TRAINING, STAKING AND TYING; HEDGES

just as cold a few hours later. This see-saw in temperature causes severe Mildew as well as making growth difficult. One should always try to avoid great variations of temperature.

While permanent materials may define a boundary, a living hedge makes the best frame for a beautiful garden. If plants are used they should be considered from the angle of upkeep, such as the frequency of cutting required, height control and especially root run. A troublesome but worth-while operation is to sink an asbestos sheet edgewise below soil level between the hedge and the rose bed. Otherwise the cooler and richer soil may attract the hedge roots and create fierce competition with the roses. Roses as hedges are dealt with elsewhere (see pages 83–84).

Except in times of extreme drought, watering of established plants should not be necessary. If watering is done it should be in dull weather or in the evening. 'Damping down' is bad. The beds should be given a heavy soaking. Begin at one end, and if time is available, direct the hose at the plants, constricting the end of the hose so that the water can be applied quite forcibly to the foliage. This will refresh the whole bush and dash to the ground greenfly and other pests. Move slowly up the border or beds, but allow time for a second watering on the return journey. The first application will prepare the dry earth and the second dose will soak in.

A heavy hose can be a lethal weapon in careless hands. A garden fork placed upright well away from the rose bed may be used as a fulcrum when pulling the pipe round the edge of the bed as its range is extended. So often the end plants are damaged as the hose swings out of control.

Seldom but thoroughly should be the rule when watering. It is unlikely that the soil content will be unbalanced in England as a result of watering. The roses which suffer most often from insufficient water are those planted close to a wall, tree or post sheltered from the prevailing summer rain winds (usually from the north-west). In such a case it is advisable to sink a 5-in. flower-pot level with the soil and about 18 in. from the root. The pot is left empty until used for watering. By filling this the water percolates directly to the root when an application to the surface would probably run off, to enter the soil finally too far from the root to be of use (see fig. 7).

One must remember that rose trees which carry seed-pods may be much exhausted in the process and flowering will be delayed or prevented. Always remove the old flower-heads. These are best cut away just above the first fully formed leaf. It is from this axil that a new shoot should arise.

If artificial manures are fed to the bushes, this should be done when the soil is moist. If it is dry, watering should be done before application and again after completing the task. Strong doses of artificial fertilizer under dry conditions can cause the plants to collapse.

When the bush begins to grow after pruning, the growth will be variable for a while. Some shoots will grow quickly, others hardly at all. After a few weeks the foliage will even out and as the leaves unfold the result of pruning will be seen. A few varieties cause confusion by the number of shoots which come from the pruned 'eyes'. Elsewhere we have noted that not only is there the large growth bud in the centre of the 'eye' but there are also two smaller 'guard eyes' which are there for emergency if the main 'eye' is damaged (see fig. 8). These three 'eyes' sometimes all grow at once and may lead to overcrowding. Try rubbing away the two guard 'eyes' when they have developed 1-in. long growths. This will give the centre shoot from the main growth bud more room to develop and more food.

TRAINING, STAKING AND TYING; HEDGES

Much is written about rose trees as hedges and one often sees rose trees offered as hedges at an extremely low price. These are usually the wild type of roses grown by the million as 'stocks' on which the modern rose trees are worked. This offer may include the common dog briar, consisting of malformed roots useless for the nurseryman, or multiflora, another seedling stock which in time can produce a massive thicket. Their market price is between one or two pence each. Nowhere is it more true than here that one gets the value one pays for.

But rose hedges of the right type can be a delight, providing a long period of flower. It is a mistake to consider such a hedge as a substitute for permanent boundary marks, but they may well define those boundaries to the eye and form a pleasing barrier to the outer world and a delightful frame to the garden within.

I have spoken of the special pruning needed—one has to choose varieties with care. A variation in height is possible but there is much to be said for keeping a hedge to one variety to ensure the unity of outline which is so important in such a position. Mixed hedges are a mixed blessing and often result in a ragged outline. The favourite where a height of 4–6 ft. is required is the Queen Elizabeth but this cultivar does have all its flower on the top and if room permits a second row on the inside made of a shorter variety may take off the rather monotonous first yard of foliage. Another very lovely pink for this purpose is Dainty Maid which stands all weathers and is for a 3–5 ft. hedge. In reds Fervid or Scarlet Queen Elizabeth, in yellows Lady Sonia or Chinatown, in orange flame Fred Loads or Orange Sensation, in white Iceberg are to be recommended.

Where a taller hedge 6–8 ft. is required some species such as Canary Bird, or rugosa hybrids, are excellent while a Musk such as Prosperity, Cornelia or Buff Beauty makes an informal screen. The ground should be especially well prepared and usually a single row is sufficient. It is advisable to plant all these fairly closely, at about a yard apart, to avoid bare gaps at the base.

If one is prepared to use some support, which should always be unobtrusive, then perpetual climbers and ramblers can be used with excellent effect. It should be borne in mind that black netting is less obtrusive than green.

Such hedges may well be the only opportunity for the owner of a small garden to have a number of one sort, so that suitability for cutting should be considered.

So we come to the close of the second section. First the root, the sure foundation. Secondly the shoot, the pleasing framework. Both essential preparation for the final glory. Even so it will be strange if we have not absorbed much of the beauty and charm of the growing plant. Its many tinted leaves, its varying thorns, the individuality of the growing plants, as different in their looks and habits as a lusty group of thriving children, will fill us with keen anticipation for the glorious culmination.

PART III

The Flower and the Bush

7
Rose Blooms: How to Identify and Treat Them

If the reader has been sufficiently patient to get as far as this, his persistence should be rewarded as we consider the crowning glory of the rose. By now I hope he has realized that this book is in the right order. Firstly roots, secondly shoots and now thirdly the flowering bush.

What is striking about the flower of the rose is its great variety of structure and colour, and it may be helpful to consider very briefly why this is so.

Two main family groups are united in the modern rose. The first was found in south-eastern and eastern Asia, the second in southern Europe and south-western Asia. Those branches of the family which arose from China and neighbouring countries were largely climbers and mostly not very hardy. Somewhere hidden in the climbing strain was a dwarfing quality which at times emerged. In the wild state the dwarf roses must have appeared many times but the hazards of nature must have destroyed them. When these dwarfs were discovered by the keen Chinese gardeners of many years—possibly two thousand or more—ago, they brought them into their gardens, cultivated them and especially if the original single flowers had doubled, they propagated them, probably growing them from seed, when other dwarf varieties were selected. When these Chinese ancestors were brought into Europe they were already far removed from their wild forbears.

THE FLOWER AND THE BUSH

Possibly equally far back in time as in China, European and south-western Asian roses had been grown and selected for their perfume and beauty. While one must allow for wide variations, the tendency was for shrubby scented roses in reds with a bluish tint, purples, pinks and whites. There was a preponderance of light magenta reds.

The colours were limited to reds, both clear (from China) and dusky (from Europe), pinks, whites and mother-of-pearl containing some sulphur yellow tones (from China).

The harsh deep yellows arose at the turn of this century and the brilliant fire-orange shades have appeared during the last twenty years.

Growth varied even more than colour. The climbing type persisted in some forms and the dwarf ceased to be non-climbing shrubs and became really short. So rose bushes were found of all heights, shapes and characters.

If colour and form of bush showed great variety so did the way the flowers came. In early stages all roses on both sides were carried in clusters. All were single or semi-single and most came into flower on their two-year wood.

Because of this wide variety it is well to know something of the behaviour of each main group, and provided we remember that there are many variations, we may accept the following groupings as true in the majority of instances.

One ought to pause to consider the type of flower-head, as this must be defined to make the description intelligible.

We have seen that all rose flower-heads were multiples of flowers. These clusters were exaggerated or diminished as their purpose varied and as time progressed. The types were two. Firstly a mass of flowers which by its very quantity made a colourful mass and which being of single flowers, opened better in wet weather and so was more reliable. In this case quantity was always the objective. Secondly there were those where the quality of size and shape in the individual flower predominated. To obtain more petals in larger flowers there had to be a slowing down of production. Therefore at the other end of the scale came the large flowers, one to a stem, slowly developing and long lasting.

Now to bewilder us these two types are being welded together in the hope—vain I believe—of producing many large flowers, continuously.

It is well to carry these two pictures in our mind. Many small flowers continuously borne. A few perfect flowers carried intermittently.

Perhaps another point might be mentioned here which is of great importance. That is, the quality of the flower depends primarily on the quality of the petal.

If a flower is to last the petal must have weather resistance and be sun-proof. The quantity of petal is of far less importance. Later, when we come to consider the best types of roses for all purposes, this factor will apply to every type of rose.

After this introduction, we will seek to define the chief characteristics of the common types.

RAMBLERS

A few years ago these were easily defined. They were once-flowering tall trees which made their slender pendulous growths one year and then flowered on that wood the following year, at the same time making new growths for the succeeding years. In other words there was growth —rest—flower. These sorts had their flowers in large clusters and most of the individual blooms were on the smaller side, 2 in. across being a fair average. Later two changes took place; some became more vigorous and stiffer in growth, and because of this extra vigour secondary growths appeared, both from the base (like the early ramblers) and from farther up the one-year rod. This meant the rhythm of first-year growth, second-year flower might become first-year growth, second-year flower and growth on the same shoot. Thus pruning (see page 56) becomes more complicated.

The second change came with the perpetual rambler represented by the Kordesii group raised by that great hybridist Herr Wilhelm Kordes. This type grew and flowered in the first year, flowered and grew the second year both summer and autumn. This is why you will find ramblers divided into three types under pruning (see p. 56), but basically the type of flower even if a little bigger is the same as the rambler.

CLIMBERS

The word climber is loosely applied to at least two types. Some bush roses go back to their ancestors. This is called 'sporting' and when they do this they lose their quality of repeat flowering and dwarf character, going back to their vigorous climbing form. These climbing sports are very common and their cycle is usually growth—rest—flower, so that they flower on the wood which has grown the previous year. A smaller number only make a partial change. They climb less vigorously and will produce strong shoots which end in flower buds as well as stronger growths which flower after a winter's rest. The basic difference between a climber and a rambler is that the climber will flower quite well on the side shoots from its strong growths for some years while the true rambler will rapidly deteriorate after the first year. Just as there are Kordesii ramblers which flower more than once so there are climbers which are called perpetual. They may not be flowering all the time but they do flower over quite a long period. Before we leave this type it is as well to remember that climbing sports of a perpetual flowering floribunda are not themselves necessarily perpetual. They are mostly once flowering although a few give an occasional flower in the autumn.

Possibly this is as good a time as any to introduce the larger bush types. Some are known as old-fashioned varieties and shrub roses. They vary from strong sprawling bushes of 6 ft. to smaller compact shrubs. Most are once flowering and as they vary in their habits one will need to do a little detective work. If they flower on the tips of their shoots they will need later on to have their flower tips removed. If they flower on their two-year wood all they will need is tipping. These old-fashioned roses and species, i.e. roses directly or closely connected with wild varieties, need the same treatment when pruning is considered. Shrub roses will vary more as they tend to be more like tall bedding floribunda or bush H.T. varieties.

Now we come to the fourth type. These are the polyantha group, originating from hardy Japanese parents, which by later breeding with wider parentage became floribunda roses. There is a lot of uncertainty about defining this class but the test is simple. If the second flower is forming well before the first flower-head has finished, it may be classed as a floribunda (see fig. 16). Continuity is the proof. Without this continuity masqueraders are really creeping in where they don't belong.

Again there are two types. The original type began with small flowers in big clusters. The flowers were usually double and the second flower-head was well developed some time before the first flower was exhausted. All the art of the grower went into encouraging continuity of bloom so after a time five- to ten-petalled flowers became popular.

16. Flower-head of floribunda type

Because this type was pre-eminently suited for massing in beds its popularity became immense and many raisers sought to cash in by producing a large-flowered type of rose with the freedom of the floribunda. These became known as Floribunda H.T. type. I must repeat that a large flower with many petals takes more time to develop than a single rose, and this is very true of the Floribunda H.T. type. They are usually intermittent not continuous and it is wishful thinking and sales possibilities which put them in a continuous flowering class.

We come to the last type I think we need to describe, and these four distinct types: (1) climbers and ramblers, (2) old-fashioned and shrub roses, (3) floribunda and floribunda H.T. type, and now (4) H.T., will include by far the majority of the roses we need to know.

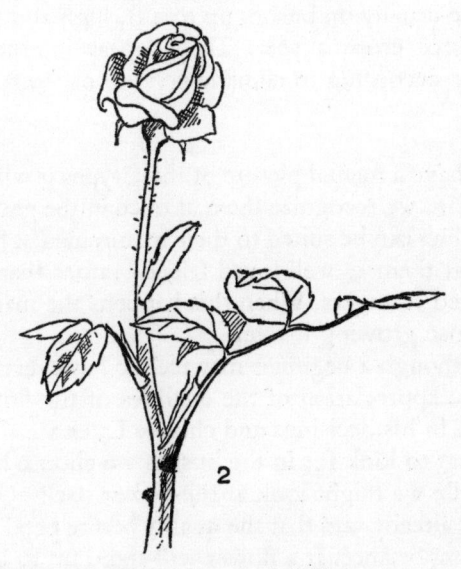

17. Flower-head of H.T. type

H.T. as a class is as meaningful or as meaningless as 'floribunda'. They are just names of convenience which convention and necessity have seized on to describe two types of roses. 'H.T.', short for hybrid tea, is half true in that hybrid it most certainly is. Mongrel, while less polite, is more true. The 'tea', like the 'Mac' or 'O' in some people's names, indicates that somewhere in the past one ancestor migrated from a different clime.

What 'hybrid tea' does indicate is a type of flower

usually consisting of a number of petals varying from five to many which have formed a full shapely bloom effective in itself. The flowers are often quite large, 5 in. across and are carried at the end of the growing stem although some other buds and flowers may cluster around them on smaller stems coming from the main branch. These H.T.s are usually on bushes up to 4 ft. high and produce up to three crops a year. They appear intermittently, flowering according to climatic conditions from June to October.

If we have a mental picture of these types it will not be long before we recognize them at once in the garden and our conduct can be suited to their requirements. Soon we shall treat them as well-loved friends rather than as unrecognized strangers. When this happens the main problem of rose growing is over.

Even though a beginner may feel he has everything to learn, the appreciation of the qualities of the flower will help him in his decisions and choice. Later we shall consider what to look for in the bushes we choose but for a little while we might look at the flower itself.

I have already said that the quality of the petal is of the utmost importance. If a flower will stand up to both sun and rain then two important assets for success have been achieved. Nothing is more depressing and disappointing than when after weeks of expectation and anticipation the swelling buds fail to open into the lovely flowers seen at the show or depicted in the catalogue. Many flowers rot in the bud or opening flower. In most cases this is due to the lack of healthy petalage. One must be sure that if such rotting occurs in the centre of a group of buds the offender is immediately removed, otherwise the whole head may succumb. A fault which is as bad, if not worse, is fading in colour. This can be really offensive when a vivid orange scarlet turns to purple magenta, as sometimes happens.

The second item of importance, especially in floribunda roses, is the spacing of flowers on a truss. If these are bunched together the centre bud may not be able to fall ('shatter' is the term used) and will remain to detract from the beauty and perfection of the remainder.

Bearing these simple facts in mind one may well go a step further. Because one is a beginner there is no reason why one should not try to exhibit at the local flower show. Indeed there are often special novice classes where only beginners may show. Some will say 'for those who have never won a prize before', others for growers of a limited number of rose bushes, but such competitions are invaluable in helping the grower to appreciate the worthwhile qualities in a rose and to seek to get the very best out of what he is doing.

My advice would be try your own local show. Obtain and read your schedule setting forth the rules to be followed. Then read again and see if there is a class especially suited to yourself. Do not try many classes, one straight competition where quality counts and one artistic attempt if this appeals to you should be your introduction to this absorbing pastime.

What type of class would be the best? If there is such a class and you have them then I would unhesitatingly suggest 'A vase of ramblers or climbers'. This is always the least competitive and generally the worst prepared class of any and yet a good exhibit may be a real contribution to the show.

There are certain basic principles which apply to all classes. The first is the exhibit should always appear young and fresh. I think this is where ramblers and climbers fail, for a large head of flower if exhibited as it has grown, may have both young and fresh, old and discoloured flowers growing together. The wise exhibitor removes spent blooms neatly and carefully. He may have to decide then whether an older flower if removed spoils the symmetry of the head. On balance it may leave such an obvious hole that it should be allowed to remain. This really moves on to the second point. The exhibit should always look natural. Even so it should look at its best. Like the careful good looks of a well-preserved lady it should be hard to tell where nature ends and art begins. Providing a bloom or blooms look natural it does not matter how much they have been aided to achieve that look. Obviously one must know one's rose and this is where exhibitions can not only provide a temporary thrill but also permanently improve our powers of observation and increase our interest. Under no circumstances should weathered petals be removed from the flower.

Another important point is that the flower should have its natural complement of healthy foliage. Added leaves are usually disqualified. If the foliage is to be worthy, it must be disease-free and unattacked by pests. This lovely foil is a natural complement to beauty and so the win on the show bench can be the reward for good husbandry.

If this foliage is to be appreciated it must be natural. One cannot exhibit a large head of a rambler perhaps 15 in. high with a leaf stem of 6 in. The stem should be proportionate and a vase of roses with good long stems well covered with healthy foliage attracts the eye of a judge even before other qualities begin to be assessed.

Young flowers, of good colour with healthy foliage well set up, will carry an exhibit if not into the winning class at least into the precincts and one need never be ashamed of such specimens.

All these rules we have applied to ramblers and climbers apply equally to any other type. A few more simple points are worth remembering. The receptacle or vase must be proportionate to the items we are showing. Three stems of ramblers are useless in a one-pound jam jar. If we are reduced to using cheap containers let them be clean and tidy. A jam jar with the maker's label adhering speaks of careless lack of preparation. A coat of neutral or black paint, put on well before the show, may make a world of difference. It is that little extra care, such as neat labelling, which can make all the difference.

A word on cutting rose blooms. The first year cut as few long stems as possible, but always remove the old dead flower-heads. In the case of marred flowers like floribundas the head as a whole may be removed when every flower has died. This should be cut to the first plump 'growth eye' which is supported by a full-sized leaf. Usually such a 'growth eye' will have already developed into a shoot. Make a clean cut just above the shoot (see fig. 11, page 55). If the dying flower offends nip off the single flower on its own short stem. Make the cut cleanly to an 'eye' you would like to grow into a strong shoot, usually facing outwards. Old H. T. flowers should have their stem removed to the first plump 'eye'. Cut your flowers for decoration if possible in the evening, or second best in the morning as soon as the dew has dried. Get your flowers into water as soon as possible and plunge the stem so that the foliage is submerged, but keep the flower quite dry. Store these containers in the coolest part of the house until morning. If you have far to take or send them, make sure that the blooms are dry, and pack them quite firmly. There should be no space left for the blooms to shake about and chafe. Pack the whole inside of the containers in polythene which should be folded over making a draught-free, and therefore moist, atmosphere for these travellers.

If you have to show at a distance and have to travel with your flowers out of water open the package as soon as you reach your destination and plunge the stems into water again submerging the leaves. Keep them there as long as you can, getting the position where you are to show, container and judging card ready before you begin on the exhibit.

While exhibiting may be for the few, indoor decoration may be for all. The rose excels in that a single flower in a simple vase may be of as rare and exquisite beauty as the ornate massing of many blossoms and much foliage by a connoisseur.

8

Choosing Your Rose Bushes

Before presenting a list of roses to be grown it might be helpful to consider what sort of a bush we should buy and why. I think most of us at heart know that we get what we pay for, but even so there is an urge within us to purchase a 'bargain'. If we buy a watch or a car we know that there is a certain range of price which guarantees a certain quality of goods. It is more difficult, especially for the beginner, to realize that the same is true in the purchase of a rose bush. A good bush is 'selected' and this means firstly that it was propagated from materials chosen especially for the purpose of getting maximum quality. Unfortunately when nature begins uniformity ceases and so, however good the original material, once propagated there will be variations. To ensure a selection of the best, not more than half of the stocks planted will produce top-size bushes. The best bushes must be grown with abundant light and air, thus taking twice the area of smaller bushes. Those which are weakly must be destroyed or sold to the cheap jack. Recently the British Standards Institution has issued certain recommendations. Briefly the definitions are: Standard Rose, a rose plant that is budded on to a stem or lateral at a height of 2 ft. or more above the ground. (Standards are usually 3 ft. 6 in., half standards 2 ft. 6 in. and weeping standards not less than 4 ft. 9 in. above the ground.) The plant must have a well-balanced head with at least two growing budded branches.

A bush shall have a balanced root and top, with a mini-

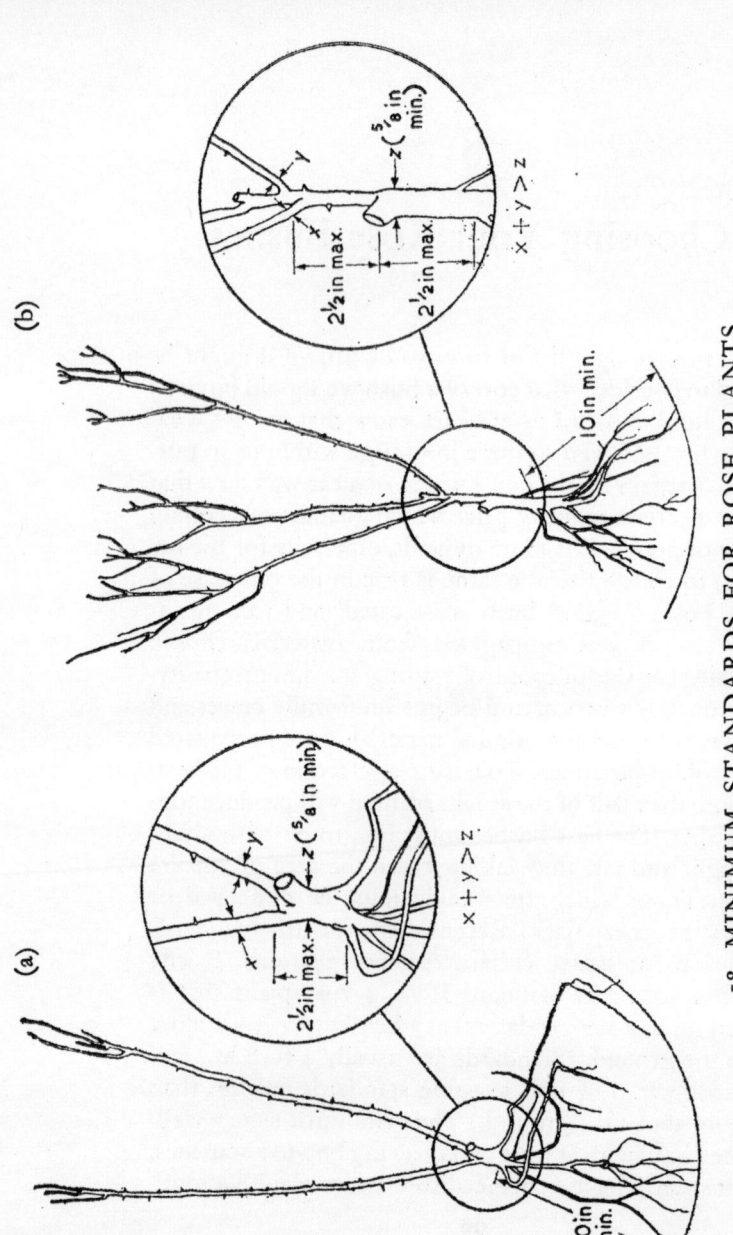

18. MINIMUM STANDARDS FOR ROSE PLANTS
(reproduced by permission of the British Standards Institution)
(a) Rose plant with two shoots arising directly from the budded union
(b) Rose plant with one shoot branching within 2½ in. of the budded union

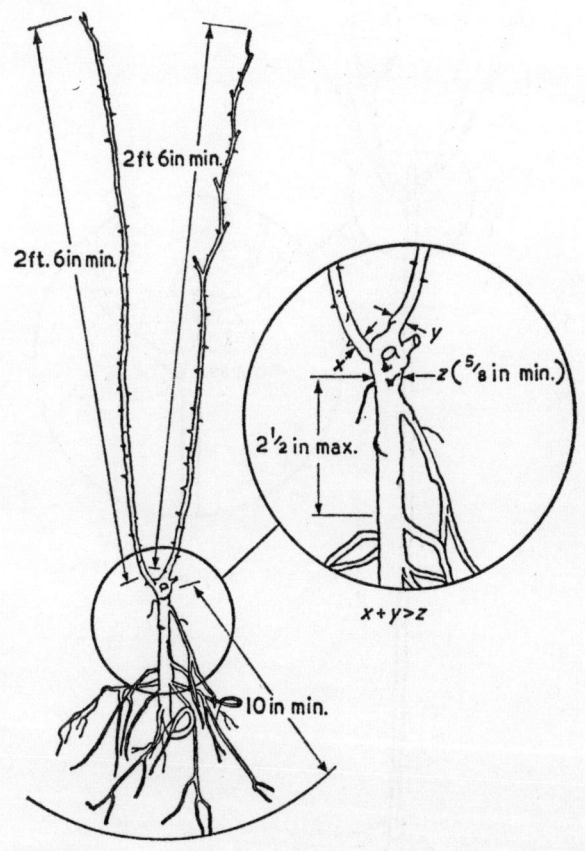

18. MINIMUM STANDARDS FOR ROSE PLANTS

(c) Climbing, rambler or pillar rose

This diagram is only intended to clarify the minimum dimensional requirements of the specification

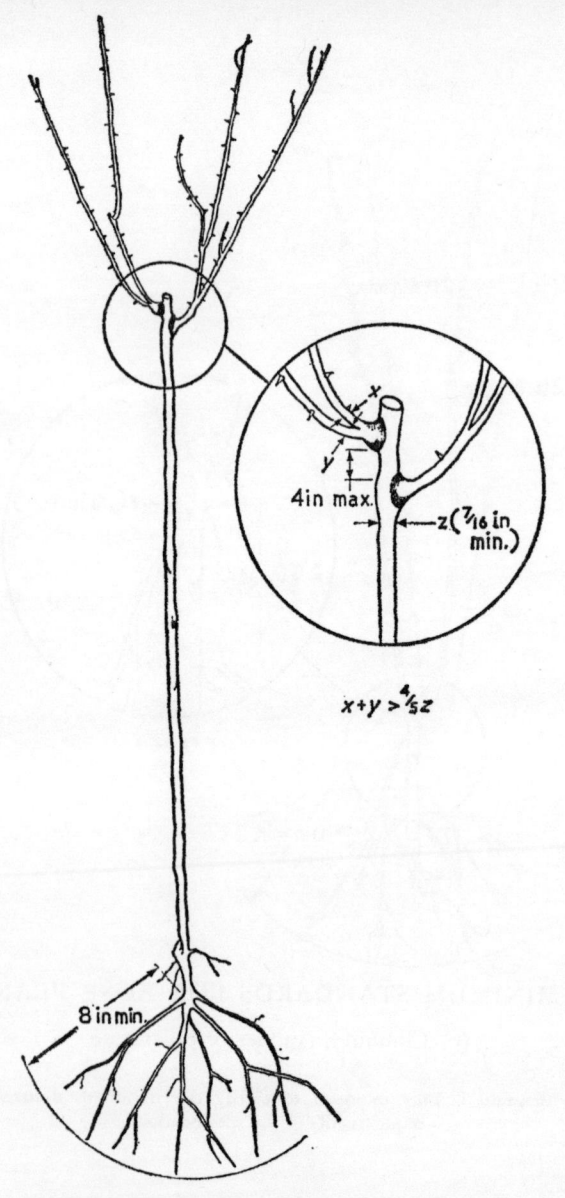

18. MINIMUM STANDARDS FOR ROSE PLANTS

(d) Standard rose

$x + y > \frac{4}{5}z$

This diagram is only intended to clarify the minimum dimensional requirements of the specification

CHOOSING YOUR ROSE BUSHES

mum of two well-ripened shoots at the union. The roots shall be a minimum of 10 in. in length. The length of shoot is immaterial providing it is over 8 in. to allow for future pruning. Most nurserymen trim the tops before despatch to save transport costs and to prevent wind-rock when planted.

A climbing or rambling rose should have a similar type of root and shoot and be cut down to not more than 2 ft. 6 in.

There are many other suggestions such as varieties being true to name, adequate labelling and health which, taken together, enable the purchaser to have confidence in the product he purchases.

Fig. 18 shows what is attempted but the rose specialist will not necessarily make this standard a final guide. For him it is a minimum and, as a specialist, he will supply the best possible bushes for that particular variety. It cannot be stressed too strongly that a high standard of bush does not produce uniformity in different varieties. A good 'Ena Harkness' need be only half the size of 'Uncle Walter'! The former grows an average of $2\frac{1}{2}$ ft., the latter 6 ft. All of what has been said comes to this. Good bushes can never be cheap to buy, for with them you obtain not only selected material but a specialist's interest and knowledge. Good roses should be an investment and should last from ten to fifteen years, improving as they age. What difference does it make in cash returns over such a period whether you chance your luck at 3s. 6d. a time or pay 6s. for the best that money can buy?

If 6s. will buy a top-size bush why pay more? There is a reason. To produce, test and market a new rose is a long and costly job and to reimburse the raiser and encourage him to seek for something better, he must be paid for this work. This has been recognized by the introduction of the Plant Varieties Act which allows a raiser to protect his new variety and to charge a royalty on all plants of that cultivar. A special label is often used to guarantee such roses to be true to name and as a proof that the royalty has been honestly paid. The royalty is small and rapidly decreases but it does ensure that the man who made the new variety possible has a fair reward. While stocks are limited a higher price is paid, for however many bushes of the one sort are raised they had to come, all of them, from the one original bush.

The time taken and the space occupied by a planted bush demands an eye to the future. Like a healthy child who reaches maturity with the minimum of illness and therefore expense, so the rose bush is a promise of future pleasure and fulfilment. There is a third reason for purchasing from specialists. Such firms cater for particular needs. It is possible to grow certain varieties in large quantities at a reduced price, but such sorts in this package deal may be quite unsuited to your needs and may well be a liability in the end.

The best and only the best provide lasting pleasure and in an emergency the specialist is ready with advice and help. Indeed he will go further and even guarantee a rose tree to bloom as well as being true to name. Personally, I think such a guarantee is unwise and unjust, and should not be taken as a prerogative with any purchase. Like any living thing, whether plant or animal, no guarantee can be given that life will be long or short, but just as an insurance company will underwrite a life, a reputable firm may be prepared to underwrite their products. If a rose tree fails it is not necessarily a reflection on the supplier. More probably it has succumbed to the means of transport or the maltreatment or neglect of the 'plantsman'. This replacement guarantee should be considered a concession not a right, and is one more reason for buying from firms with established reputations.

9
Group 1
Ramblers and Climbers

In dealing with a selection of varieties in this book it cannot be too strongly stated that the omission of a variety does not mean it is unworthy of a place in the garden. There are too many sorts to confuse the beginner. The following list has been compiled from personal knowledge, and a careful appraisement of varieties as they have been grown at the Queen Mary Rose Garden in London; the Royal National Rose Society's grounds at St. Albans; the Royal Horticultural Society's garden at Wisley; the North of England Horticultural Society's Harlow Car grounds, Harrogate and the Trial and other gardens at Roath Park, Cardiff; beside experience gained from many private gardens and my own rose field and trial grounds.

The groups are listed as they are described and in the same order as in Chapter 4, page 56, i.e. Ramblers, Climbers, Old-Fashioned and Shrub Roses, Floribundas, H.Ts. The list is brief, for it is a beginner's selection, and because some colours are less easy to grow there may be fewer of one colour than another.

RAMBLERS

The original type are once flowering on wood of the previous year's growth. These are to be commended for vigour, coverage and mass effect at one period, usually late June or early July. They have their flowering growths removed as soon as flowering is over to enable the new growths to be tied in ready for the following year. All have glossy foliage. In cases where the flowers are produced throughout the season they are marked 'P'. This is the type budded on tall stems for 'weeping standards', see Chapter 6, page 77.

Types 1 and 2 (see pages 56, 57 and 89)

Alberic Barbier. A charming cluster rose with full, miniature H.T. type flowers. The buds are yellow and fade to pure white as the blooms expand. Sweetly scented its outstanding quality is the almost evergreen foliage which gives coverage from May until January.

Albertine. Better pruned hard each year but in inaccessible positions may be left for longer. This is probably the best in this class. The flowering season is short, three weeks at the most. The flowers, which are semi-double, are carried in clusters and are orange salmon in the bud opening to salmon pink with golden base. Sweetly perfumed. The foliage is coppery red in the young stage and deep olive green when mature. Although not as persistent as 'Barbier' it would be worth growing for the ornamental qualities of the foliage alone. Type 1 and 2.

American Pillar. One hesitates to exclude this rose. It is one of the hardiest and fastest growers we have. The flowers, developed in huge clusters, are single, rosy pink with a white centre and somewhat untidy before dropping. For covering an inaccessible roof, sprawling over a tall tree or stump, or filling a draughty corner, it is unbeatable. Type 2.

GROUP I: RAMBLERS AND CLIMBERS

Crimson Shower. Raised much later than the rest in this class it has the unique feature of flowering late—the end of July or early August. Big clusters of rosy crimson flowers with very long whippy shoots. The foliage is small, plentiful and deep green. A useful variety for flowering in between seasons. Type 1.

Excelsa. Small, double, light crimson flowers in large clusters on pendulous shoots. Many long, thin, whippy growths. Better used in its weeping form. Type 1.

François Juranville. This retiring but charming beauty is in pastel shades of pink. The small double flowers are very freely produced on long slender graceful shoots. Very useful as a relief from the harsh and rather blatant modern colours. Scented. Type 2.

Minnehaha. Fully double rosette-shaped flowers in very large flower-heads of deep pink. Extremely vigorous. Type 1.

Snowflake. Pure white double flowers in large clusters on strong stems. Vigorous and very free growth. Sweetly scented. Type 1.

Veilchenblau. An old variety which is included because its colour, magenta-violet with white centre, is returning to favour. It is heavily perfumed and if the stiff rod-like stems are well trained can be made a colour feature or contrast. Light green foliage with vigorous growths. Type 2.

Chaplin's Pink. Very large semi-double, deep pink blooms borne in bewildering profusion. This magenta shaded pink is not easy to mix with any other but most effective by its sheer mass of spectacular colour. A very vigorous growth which demands careful training to induce numerous flowering shoots. One of the best for covering tall positions. Contrasts well with blue conifers. Type 2.

Chaplin's Pink Companion. Another rampant rambler producing a wealth of silvery pink double flowers. A newer and very promising variety. Type 2.

Dr. Van Fleet. Small silvery pink flowers of H.T. type in large clusters carried in great profusion on very vigorous and lengthy shoots. Both flower and perfume are outstanding in quantity and quality. The flowering season is short but memorable. A less vigorous but perpetual form is known as The New Dawn. Type 1.

Emily Gray. Deep golden buff semi-double flowers of short duration. A very lovely flower which needs a sunny position and judicious thinning of surplus wood if there are to be many flowers. The young growths are extremely handsome, their pansy purple contrasting with the deep glossy olive green mature foliage. Very vigorous. Type 2.

Paul's Scarlet Climber ('Blaze Superior' is supposed to be a more free flowering form). This bright unfading scarlet with crimson shadings produces a profusion of semi-double flowers. Growth is moderately vigorous. If the growths are allowed to mature secondary later flowers will develop on the side growths in the autumn. This will probably be superseded by the more profuse Kordesii Hybrids or Danse des Sylphes. Pruning Type 3.

Kordesii (K) and other types of perpetual ramblers

Remember these require less drastic treatment than ram-

GROUP I: RAMBLERS AND CLIMBERS

blers of types 1 and 2 and much of the wood while it remains healthy may have its long canes left, shortening the side shoots after flowering. Flowers are produced over a long period; usually there is one heavy flush followed by intermittent flowers. These vary greatly in growth. The Kordesii as a whole being vigorous, 8–10 ft., and most of the others 6–8 ft.

Altissimo (P). A very striking rambler or climber with large leathery leaves producing clusters of large almost single flowers of great brilliance and intensity. Colour deep red enlightened with a brilliant glow. Needs a really tall site when it is spectacular. Type 2.

Golden Showers (P). Long pointed bud opening to full, flat, fragrant, daffodil yellow flower carried singly and in clusters. Foliage dark and glossy. Growth 6–8 ft. Useful for low walls or trellises. Type 3.

Leverkusen (K). A less vigorous member, 6–8 ft. The flowers are large, double yellow, carried in clusters. Light green glossy foliage. Type 3.

Maigold (P). A hybrid briar. One of the best but different in growth being very thorny. The large, deep, almost orange-yellow, semi-double flowers are very fragrant and are borne freely, early in the season. Afterwards flowers appear on the secondary growths. Type 3.

Mermaid (P). This unique hybrid from *R. braceteata* excels at autumn flowering and therefore grows late in the season. Because of this it should be in a warm sheltered position. The flowers (like white water lilies) last for a day but are produced on their short stems in great profusion over a long period finishing with a burst of late autumn bloom. Should not be pruned beyond removing dying or unhealthy growth. Can be very tall when established.

New Dawn (P). The short perpetual type of Dr. Van Fleet (see page 108). The soft shell-pink flowers are sweetly perfumed and continue over a very long period. Ideal as a short climber or trained as a hedge with slight support. Type 3.

Park Director Riggers (K) (P). Very vigorous with large clusters of velvety crimson, pointed, slightly fragrant, medium-sized flowers. The foliage is dark green and leathery. Noteworthy in autumn as in summer. Type 3.

Ritter Von Barmstede (K) (P). Two-inch, deep pink, semi-double flowers in large clusters. The foliage is glossy and the blossoms are borne in great profusion. Type 3.

Zephirine Drouhin (P). Because of its smaller H.T. type flowers carried in clusters I have placed this cultivar here. The flowers are deep pink and are extremely sweetly scented. Useful as a short climber or tall hedge. Type 3.

CLIMBERS

This section may be divided into three sorts. First, those which have 'sported', i.e. the variety began as a bush and then a climbing form appeared. They came mostly from Hybrid Teas (H.T.s), in which case the flowers would be large. Many are once flowering, some (marked P) give autumn flower on their older wood. The other major type are climbing forms of floribundas (marked Fl.) which again usually flower once only. Third, a few varieties have

GROUP I: RAMBLERS AND CLIMBERS

been bred as climbers and as they often flower more than once have been marked P. Pruning all these as Type 2 (see pages 58 and 59).

Allgold (Fl.). Very vigorous, needs plenty of room, light and air. Fan trained it can give many flowers. Only thin overcrowded shoots. Unfading golden yellow.

Autumn Sunlight (P). A charming double, well formed flower in golden orange. One of the best both for colour and growth.

Aloha (P). Full, double, large, deep pink blooms. Short, stiff, erect growth. A slow growth but a good pillar rose about 6 ft. tall.

Casino (P). Pale yellow, vigorous and free.

Crimson Glory (H.T.). Dark vinous red, scented. Better on a west wall as flowers burn in full sun.

Danse de Feu (P). Brilliant orange red. Clusters of full H.T.-type flowers opening rather loosely. Deserves inclusion whenever possible. Vigorous.

Danse de Sylphes (P). Like a slightly larger, more perpetual Paul's Scarlet and as such deserves consideration.

Ellinor Le Grice (P) (H.T.). Large, full, deep, unfading yellow. Medium height.

Ena Harkness (H.T.). Bright red, an ideal form in which to grow this rose as the blooms hang their heads and are thus seen to perfection.

Flaming Sunset (P) (H.T.). A two-toned rose in yellow flushed scarlet.

Gloire de Dijon (P). This old favourite has very full fragrant flowers, buff pink shaded orange. One must not expect either the size, shape or clarity of colour found in modern roses.

Golden Dawn (P) (H.T.). Primrose yellow, full and very fragrant flowers on a short sturdy plant.

Guinee (P). Small H.T. flowers in blackish maroon. Sweetly scented, it is vigorous and free.

High Noon (P). An elongated bush rose which flowers at the end of its shoots then continues upward on a side shoot covering 6–8 ft. The flowers are pointed and deep yellow.

Korona (Fl.). Orange scarlet full flowers in large clusters.

Lady Sylvia (H.T.). Very vigorous covering up to 20 ft. Flowering once a year it yields a prodigious quantity of flowers with a strong penetrating perfume. An ideal rose for a tall wall.

Masquerade (Fl.). Yellow spashed red, fading salmon. The small blooms in large clusters give a spectacular display in June.

Meg (P). A semi-climber with large semi-double flowers of great charm in coral shaded peach. Suitable for a low wall or tall hedge.

Mme G. Staechelin (H.T.). A unique rose of subtle charm.

Rosa gallica versicolor (Rosa Mundi)

Rosa Filipes 'Kiftsgate'

GROUP I: RAMBLERS AND CLIMBERS

The large H.T. type buds open to semi-double clear pink flowers with a slight scarlet stain on the outer edge of the petal. A vigorous growth with slender trailing shoots it gives wide coverage. A sweet and pleasing perfume.

Mrs. Sam McGredy (H.T.). Coppery orange fading to salmon. The exquisite flowers are produced in profusion. The coppery red of the young foliage gives added charm in contrast to the deep green of the older leaf. Very vigorous, it should be given not less than 15 ft. run of space.

Parade (P). Deep rose pink full of flowers, very freely produced over a long period. It needs time to mature but flowers from the early stage.

Peace (H.T.). This is included for warning only. Some climbers are over vigorous, giving little or no flower, while growing too strongly. Climbing 'Peace' is one such, and should never be grown in Britain, although in hotter climates it flowers freely.

Pink Perpetué (P). This is one of the very best. Free in growth and flower, the full, scented flowers, clear pink with deeper reverse of petal, are attractive throughout the growing season.

Royal Gold (P). Deep golden yellow with large H.T. type flowers. It prefers a sheltered position when it can be one of the best.

Shot Silk (P). This old variety is at its best in the climbing form, when it flowers freely in autumn as in summer. Pink with golden centre, it is sweetly scented.

Soldier Boy (P). Large single flowers in unfading bright red. Always in flower from May until October. One of the few really vigorous perpetual climbers. A lovely companion for 'Mermaid' (page 109).

Spek's Yellow (P). This is a useful deep yellow cultivar where height and continuity of flower are important.

Sweet Sultan (P). Huge scarlet, shaded maroon, single flowers carried in small clusters on vigorous stout growths, clothed with tough, deep green foliage. Excellent as a short climber, a vigorous specimen bush or a tall hedge.

William Allen Richardson (P). Small, double, fragrant, pale buff yellow to apricot yellow blooms. Vigorous and free. An old Noisette giving quite different effects to the modern rose.

10

Group 2
Old-Fashioned Roses, Species and Shrubs

One is tempted to produce a massive list of older varieties which even then would be but a very tiny part of the thousands of cultivars introduced during the nineteenth century, especially during the latter half. But in a book for beginners I would suggest caution at first, not because these roses are unworthy of a place but because the average garden of the beginner today is a very small plot bought at a cost which until recently would have purchased acres of ground. If this is so then each plant must give its maximum value for as long as possible. Many of the older sorts were once flowering for a short period. Of the few suggested, most, although representative of their type and growth, flower freely for such types.

Their approximate dimensions when mature are given, width first and height second, so that they may be grown naturally. Some, especially the species, resent pruning and apart from exhausted wood should have little removed. A tall ungainly shoot may be shortened to prevent wind damage (see page 54). Marked s for scent, ss for strong scent and sss for very strong scent.

Blanc Double de Coubert (ss). The semi-single paper white, sweetly scented 3-in. flowers are carried on a stiff, erect

THE FLOWER AND THE BUSH

thorny bush. The buds come in short-stemmed clusters which flower over a long period. A hybrid from *R. rugosa*. 3 ft. × 4 ft.

Cardinal de Richelieu (sss). When fully developed, a massive double purple flower with flecks of white especially at the petal base, on a bush 5 ft. × 4 ft. with green wood and a few thorns. It is of *gallica* parentage.

Canary Bird is a delightful hybrid of species with all the best qualities of this type under garden limitations, i.e. beauty of form, compactness of growth, freedom of flower and pleasing foliage. The small, dense, fern-like foliage is carried on arching shoots laden in May with a brilliant mass of clear golden single 2-inch flowers. The rounded bush produces a few flowers on the twiggy shoots throughout the summer. In autumn the foliage turns bright yellow before falling. A bush 6 ft. × 7 ft. needing full development room.

Cecile Brunner. One of the first 'Poly-poms' the forerunners of the floribunda roses. The blooms may be carried singly or later on in the autumn on loosely formed heads of exquisite miniature H.T. shaped flowers which are a combination of pink and apricot in subdued pastel shades. 3 ft. × 3 ft. Much used for miniature decorations.

R. centifolia cristata (ss). Although this is not in the 'Moss Rose' section it has a heavily mossed effect with the clear pink buds peeping through a veil of heavily mossed calyx. A charming flower with character. 3 ft. × 4 ft.

Mme Pierre Oger (ss). A full, double, rounded ball of bloom with its open side, as if sliced flat to reveal the crowded petals. Pale creamy white with variable pink

GROUP 2: OLD-FASHIONED ROSES

tinge. Carried in small clusters and singly on a shrub-like bush. 4 ft. × 6 ft. Many autumn flowers.

R. Moyesii 'Geranium'. Quite a different group, noteworthy for the unusual orange-red single flowers carried in June and succeeded by very large urn-shaped hips which ripen in August–September. The leaves and stiff growth are quite characteristic. The cultivar 'Geranium' is more compact than the much taller *Moyesii*. 4 ft. × 6 ft.

Roger Lamberlin. A characteristic old 'Hybrid Perpetual' with rounded outline, flat flower and massed petals. The flowers are carmine-crimson flecked and edged with white and are borne freely on a smaller bush. 3 ft. × 4 ft.

R. rubrifolia. This is the red-leaved species used for its decorative foliage. The younger wood is almost thornless and plum purple. The flowers are insignificant, being little grouped tufts of pink and white succeeded by many rounded bright red hips. The size is better controlled by fairly hard pruning as it is the young shoot which is most ornamental, in which case there will be fewer fruit. 4 ft. × 6 ft.

Schneezwerg (ss) (Snow Dwarf). A compact bush carrying a mass of semi-single 2½-in. white blooms, sweetly scented and bearing numerous small red hips which mingle with the autumn flowers. A hybrid *rugosa*. 2 ft. × 3 ft.

Versicolor (*R. gallica versicolor* also known as *Rosa mundi*) (sss). One of the best known older roses carrying a great profusion of semi-single large flowers, carmine striped on a pale pink background. 3 ft. × 4 ft.

A few Shrub Roses

While some vigorous H.T. type and floribunda roses make excellent specimens, Peace, Uncle Walter, Buccaneer, Queen Elizabeth and Dainty Maid being good examples, there are others which at all times should be treated as strong growing shrubs. For pruning, see pages 60 and 62.

Ballerina. A very unusual small single flower in huge clusters of pink and white blossom. The foliage is small also but the effect is delightful. About 4 ft. high and as much in diameter.

Bonn. One of the modern Hybrid Musks. A tall, 7-ft. shrub, flowering over a long period with large trusses of semi-single red flowers.

Buff Beauty (ss). A large, long, conical head of double, perfumed, buff flowers on arching shoots making a sturdy bush of some 5 ft. × 5 ft. A long flowering season. One of the best Hybrid Musks.

Fred Loads. A tall, brilliant, orange-scarlet single flower in very large clusters on strong upright stems. Vigorous and healthy. 6 ft. × 4 ft.

First Choice. A brilliant bi-colour that is scarlet inside the petal with golden reverse. The large pointed buds open rapidly into nearly single flowers. A most effective splash of colour. 5 ft. × 5 ft.

Lady Sonia. Deep yellow, full flowers with strong, healthy and sturdy growth. A very useful shrub in a change of colour.

GROUP 2: OLD-FASHIONED ROSES

These present a few of the many but unless the beginner has a large garden these shrubs must be limited as to position. Where a large area has to be covered these and many more can be used with great effect but they need ample space.

11

Group 3
The Floribunda Roses

The Floribunda Roses (see fig. 16, page 92) are not easy to define but there are two main factors. The first is succession of bloom. The flower-heads vary in size and shape, but their most definite factor is that while the shoot is bearing flowers another growth is already breaking from the first leaf bud just below the flower-head so that the period of waiting between flowering is very short. The second is quantity of blooms on each head. This varies also but there are many more flowers on the average head than with the H.T. group. The third factor is the form of the flower itself. Where quantity is greatest the flowers are either five-petalled singles, semi-doubles or small double flowers. These I think should be considered the true floribundas. At the moment another type, the floribunda H.T. type, is recognized. These have large flowers with the shape of H.T. roses, and in most cases the centre bud is considerably larger than the side buds. Because it takes longer for a large flower to mature, and because this type has been bred near the H.T., the secondary flower shoots are less abundant and the flower-heads smaller. It is really a question of quantity versus quality. As a rule floribunda roses are grown for massing and therefore the true floribunda roses produce the most effective mass and usually suffer less from wet weather.

Because these are used for bedding effect, height is of

GROUP 3: THE FLORIBUNDA ROSES

great importance but it must be understood very clearly that the heights given are relative and will vary greatly under different conditions of soil and climate.

Those marked (H) have everywhere proved to be easy to grow and satisfactory in flower and foliage.

RED

Floribunda Roses

Dusky Maiden (ss) (H). A true single with deep velvety red blooms, the golden anthers of which lighten the whole flower. Sweetly perfumed, it is very free flowering, with large, deep green, healthy foliage. Remove old flowers to prevent seed pods forming. Height 2–2½ ft.

Europeana (ss). A very striking variety with large heads of double, brilliant red flowers. Especially noteworthy is the dark reddish purple young foliage. The heavy heads tend to make the plants sprawl, but closely planted (18 in. apart) the bushes support one another. Some Black Spot and Mildew. Height 2–3 ft.

Evelyn Fison. A very brilliant scarlet red with shapely buds, opening into pleasing flowers on a large upright head. The colour is maintained. An excellent bedding rose of healthy, pleasing growth. Height 2–2½ ft.

Fervid (H). A tall, erect growth, especially useful for large beds or hedges. The semi-single flowers with waved petals are carried on massive heads of brilliant unfading red of remarkable intensity. Especially good on light sandy soils. Height 3½–4 ft.

Firecrest (H). One of the most consistently free-flowering cultivars we have. Remarkably uniform in height, it flowers from early to late with large well-spaced heads of full pointed orange red flowers. The colour remains good except in the hottest of suns. Good for cutting and is brilliant under artificial light. Height 2 ft.

Frensham. For years one of the best and most popular crimson red varieties. Very heavy foliage and massive growth marred by its propensity for Mildew. Makes a good hedge in good soil in an open position. Height $3\frac{1}{2}$–4 ft.

Lili Marlene (H). A rose of great merit and charm. The large semi-single blooms are clear red with deep, almost black, shading. A little spare in foliage, which is, however, healthy. Ideal for bedding. Height 2–$2\frac{1}{2}$ ft.

Marlena. The shortest of the red varieties. Very free flowering and compact. Ideal for use as a dwarf. Height 1–$1\frac{1}{2}$ feet.

Meteor. Brilliant orange-red with 2- to 3-in. blooms. Of branching habit it is to be recommended for its short growth, although the smaller flowered Marlena may be more suited to really dwarf beds it is not quite as vivid. Height $1\frac{1}{2}$–2 ft.

Sarabande (H). Another bright red with single flowers carried in large trusses on short sturdy stems. Maintaining its colour in all weathers it is one of the most trouble-free, effective and perpetual bedding roses. It has an excellent bedding effect as its growth is even and healthy. Height 2 ft.

GROUP 3: THE FLORIBUNDA ROSES

Floribunda H.T. type

Scarlet Queen Elizabeth (H). A tall almost orange-red, large 4-in. flowers carried singly and in larger heads. Sometimes the very free foliage overwhelms the flower. Too big for the small garden except as a specimen bush. Height 4 ft.

PINK

Although there are many claimants for this sector, it is only in the salmon and gold shades where varieties jostle one another for supremacy.

Floribunda Roses

City of Leeds. 3½-in. semi-double blooms of rich salmon. Vigorous upright growth. The large flower-heads are freely produced. Height 2½–3 ft.

Dainty Maid. One of the single-flowered type which withstands all weathers. The inner side of the petal is clear pink with deeper reverse, with all the fresh charm of the wild briar. Excellent for beds or as a hedge. Height 3½ ft.

Elizabeth of Glamis (sss). This lovely light salmon flower is weather resistant and sweetly perfumed. Of free growth and good health it has one grave fault in that it transplants badly, and is not happy on heavy cold soils where its life is short. It is so good in some places that it should not be universally condemned, but all cold positions, especially frost pockets, should be avoided. Height 2–2½ ft.

Ma Perkins. Full 2-in. flowers of pale blush pink carried in large clusters on a short but sturdy plant. Height 1½–2 ft.

Pernille Poulsen (s). A cheerful clear deep pink. The loose 4-in. flowers are carried in great profusion on the first crop with rather a long wait for the second flowering. Some fragrance. A compact and pleasing bedding variety. Height 2 ft.

Plentiful. A unique deep pink, very double bloom carried in huge clusters. The petals drop cleanly, one of its many assets as a good bedding rose. Better planted closely, to give support to its large flower-heads. Growth healthy and free. Height 2–2½ ft.

Posy. This little rose is almost short enough for a miniature. Most profuse in 2-in. double lilac-pink flowers. It should be planted at 15-in. spacing. A charm and purpose of its own with its upright 15 in. of growth.

Sweet Repose (s). I was inclined to place this in the H.T. group for its exquisite buds are highly decorative. Carried singly or many on a stem it is one of those roses where the colours deepen and change with age. A confection of cream, amber and pink early, it changes to crimson and white in the older flower. At all times very lovely. A taller grower not quite so good for bedding, but a lovely specimen. Height 2½–3 ft.

Floribunda H.T. type

Chanelle (H). One of my favourites. A blend of pastel shades with amber and shell pink vying for supremacy. The very large healthy leaves make an excellent foil for

GROUP 3: THE FLORIBUNDA ROSES

its many blossoms. A restful relief amid the blatant brilliance of the modern roses.

Dearest. Salmon pink, large H.T. type flowers. Very lovely at its best but dislikes rain and should not be planted where rust is prevalent.

Innisfree (H). Included for its health, especially resistance to Black Spot. A variable colour changing from orange-yellow to pearl. The flowers are moderately full 2-in., with vigorous branching growth. Height 2½–3 ft.

Paddy McGredy. An unusual bush, carrying on its short sturdy shoots many large H.T.-type flowers. Beginning as red buds they fade rapidly on opening to a rather dingy pink. To avoid disease plant in industrial areas only. Height 1½–2 ft.

Salmon Sprite (sss). Deep salmon, full, miniature H.T.s carried singly and in clusters on tall upright stems. Intense perfume. Promising for bedding. A little late with its second crop of flowers. Height 2–2½ ft.

Sea Pearl. A lovely mixture of pinks with a yellow petal base. At times the large flowers remind one of an H.T. in their limited crop but the strong upright autumn shoots will carry a full crop of good flowers. Height 3–3½ ft.

Pink Parfait. A mass of small H.T. blooms in a delightful combination of pale and deeper pinks. The tall upright growth is healthy and crowned with large flower-heads. Like all these fuller types there is a considerable wait for more flowers but a large bed in its first flush is an unforgettable sight. Height 3–3½ ft.

Scented Air (ss). Like 'Innisfree' abounding in health. The vivid salmon flowers are almost orange at first but fade on opening to a more subdued but pleasing pink. Sweetly scented. Height 2–2½ ft.

Queen Elizabeth (H). Should not be considered in this class but unless we delegate it to the shrubs, it must be found a home somewhere for the wealth of long-stemmed, clear pink, full H.T.-sized blooms are useful for decoration. Very vigorous, it may be grown as a hedge or specimen bush. It needs to be planted in the background, for unless great care is used in pruning, the first 3 ft. of the bush is uninteresting, for often both foliage and flower as lacking at the base of the plant. Do not mix with assorted floribundas.

ORANGE

Included here are both the orange scarlet and their softer-toned fellows.

Anna Wheatcroft. A short growth with large clusters of single vermilion flowers. A unique shade with considerable appeal. Height 2½ ft.

Circus. Short and sturdy with full pointed flowers of orange shaded apricot paling a little on opening. A healthy growth with an abundance of flower. Height 2 ft.

Copper Delight (ss). A delightful 'self' colour between gold and orange. The graceful 3-in. flowers are sweetly scented and make an attractive foil for the more harsh orange-scarlets. Pointed shapely buds opening wide to semi-double flowers. Better planted in industrial areas or kept

GROUP 3: THE FLORIBUNDA ROSES

carefully sprayed to avoid Black Spot. Height 1½–2 ft.

Fairlight. Deep coppery scarlet, veined scarlet, paling on opening. Large flat heads of semi-double flowers. Excellent for bedding. An interesting and pleasing colour. Height 2–2½ ft.

Golden Slippers (s). A small, rather weakly grower but unique in its colours—tangerine with golden reverse. Altogether charming and unusual and deserves care. Fragrant. Height 1–1½ ft.

Korona. The full rather ragged trusses of orange scarlet flowers are carried upright on strong vigorous stems. This has proved to be one of the most consistent, hardy and carefree bedding roses of all time. Height 2½–3½ ft.

Princess Michiko. Large heads of single flowers, vivid coppery orange on opening, which swiftly change to a dull red. Its variability and unsightly seed pods are against it, but at its best a most delightful bedding rose. Height 2–2½ ft.

Vesper (H). A unique pastel shade of light golden brown, the large and small clusters contain many double H.T.-shaped flowers. Foliage is healthy and abundant. Ideal for flower arrangers, also good for bedding. Height 2½–3 ft.

Zambra. Brilliant orange shaded yellow. Not a good growth, being liable to Black Spot and Mildew. It is short and sturdy and a better bush, in my opinion, than the gawky 'Woburn Abbey' which seems even more prone to disease. It is the brightest colour we have in orange-vermilion. Height 1–1½ ft.

Floribunda H.T. type

Orange Sensation (sss). A wonderful rose in growth and freedom of flower, thrusting up a heavy crop in autumn as well as abundant flowers in the summer. The orange-scarlet well-formed flowers are heavily perfumed and are carried in huge trusses of small-leaved stems. Height 2½–3½ ft.

Woburn Abbey. See 'Zambra', which is the lesser of the two evils for health, but both of interesting colour.

YELLOW

Allgold (s) (H). Many flowers of deep unfading gold. Unique, almost total resistance to Black Spot. The best yellow of short growth. Height 1½–2 ft.

Golden Treasure. Brilliant golden yellow trusses with upright stems having deep green foliage. Prone to Black Spot and 'die back'. Height 2–2½ ft.

Goldgleam (s) (H). Large well-formed buds opening into semi-double flowers of deep clear yellow. Foliage healthy and abundant. Excellent for bedding. Height 2–2½ ft.

Gold Marie. When first in flower this is a tall golden yellow without equal. The older flowers are tinted salmon and there is some untidiness in the old flower on the plant. It is not very free after its first magnificent crop. Height 2½–3 ft.

There are no H.T. types worth noting although 'Arthur Bell' might deserve a place but for its habit like many others of fading white in the older flower.

Goldgleam (floribunda)

Superior (floribunda)

Virgo (H.T.)

Pink Favourite (H.T.)

GROUP 3: THE FLORIBUNDA ROSES

WHITE

Dairy Maid (ss). A single-flowered cluster rose of great charm. The buds are pale yellow stained scarlet, opening to bold trusses of white flowers. They need their flower-heads removing as soon as the flower fades. Height 2–2½ ft.

Dimples (ss). A full, many-flowered plant carrying large trusses of unusual white flowers with clear creamy yellow centres. The foliage is glossy. A pleasing foil to more brilliant flowers. Height 2–2½ ft.

Iceberg (s) (H). Pure white buds carried in large wide-spaced trusses on spreading growths. The small glossy leaves are widely spread on smooth green wood. The older flowers sometimes weather pink in a wet season. Tall and free. Height 3–3½ ft.

MAUVE

Africa Star. Lilac in bud and full bloom. Clusters on a sturdy bush. Foliage pleasing. Slow with its second crop but good although very prone to get Black Spot and also some Mildew. Height 1½–2 ft.

Lilac Charm (ss) (H). The lilac-mauve buds open to single flowers with lovely red and gold anthers. Some fading but a great abundance of repeat bloom. The bush is sturdy, short and healthy. Height 1½–2 ft.

BI-COLOURED AND MIXED

Masquerade. Probably the first and forerunner of a mighty host. A mixture of reds, pinks and golds depending on the stage of the flowers. Large clusters very freely produced. A carrier of virus, this does not affect its vigorous growth. Height 3–3½ ft.

Paintbox. Of similar type to the above with larger flowers and more upright sturdy growth. A little more regular in flowering but a little dowdy at times. More healthy than many hence its preference to the Black Spot ridden 'Charleston', which latter may be grown safely in industrial areas. Height 2½–3 ft.

Telstar. Orange-yellow heavily flushed scarlet with age. Semi-double 3½-in. flowers. Growth moderately vigorous, tall and branching. Height 3–3½ ft.

Floribunda H.T. type

Shepherdess. Yellow flushed pale salmon, semi-double 3-in. fragrant flowers. Growth vigorous and free. Height 3–3½ ft.

Polyantha Roses. These have small button-type flowers which are produced over a long season. My advice would be for the beginner to forget what is largely an outmoded type. Their greatest importance lay in their being the forerunner of the 'Poulsen' type Hybrid Polyanthas, which expanded into the Floribunda Roses of today. Much addicted to Mildew especially in the autumn.

12

Group 4
Hybrid Tea Roses

As with all classes of roses there has been much interbreeding, with the result that some H.T.s and some floribundas with larger flowers might be interchangeable as to class. Especially true is the fact that many behave as H.T.s in their first flowering, producing large flowers one to the stem, and in the autumn many flowers on one stem. If one remembers the true definition of the floribunda, i.e. a secondary growth and flower shoot being formed while the first head is blooming, the answer will be found.

In the list that follows, colour grouping has been used. Many popular varieties have been omitted as they fail to comply with the health test. Those particularly resistant to disease have been marked H; s ss and sss indicates strength of perfume.

S = Short growth 1½–2 ft.
M = Medium growth 2–3 ft.
T = Tall growth 3 ft. and up

These heights are approximate and may vary with cultural differences

LIGHT RED OR PINKY RED

Fragrant Cloud (sss). This rose might equally be classified under any of the three headings which follow, for its colour varies from a rich smoky almost vinous red to pinky red, while in hot sunshine the old flowers may turn purple. Under normal conditions it is outstandingly good, although in autumn almost too many flowers appear on one head at a time. Its perfume and growth are exceptional. M.

Wendy Cussons (sss) (H). An easy rose to grow providing large well-formed full blooms. The flowering is not as free as the growth but a very satisfying plant for many purposes. T.

GLOWING RED

Champs Elysées (H). An excellent bedding rose providing many cup-shaped brilliant blooms on a compact heathy bush. A trouble-free variety, producing quantity with colourful effect. S.

Ernest H. Morse (sss) (H). A clear brilliant red, well-formed pointed flower on an erect tall bush. In hot weather the colour fades, but few cultivars are more rewarding for growth and flower. Very free. T.

Ena Harkness (ss). Deep glowing red, full flowers of exhibition form. The developed flower hangs its head but it is free in flower and growth. M.

Konrad Adenauer (sss). A full flower of brilliant red with deeper overshades. The growth is compact, free and reliable. One of the most satisfactory for bedding effect. M.

Numero Un. Large semi-double flowers in brilliant orange-scarlet which do not fade. The growth is healthy and the foliage handsome. A bedding rose of vivid effectiveness. T.

GROUP 4: HYBRID TEA ROSES

DARK RED

Chrysler Imperial (sss) (H). Rich dark red with deeper shading. The full flower is carried upright on a stiff stem. The foliage is healthy and plentiful. M.

Ellen Mary (sss) (H). An unusual colour, rich vinous red, shapely blossoms filled with fragrance. The growth is strong and branching with healthy and abundant foliage. T.

Mme L. Laperrière (sss) (H). A very good bedding rose producing a mass of short-stemmed full and shapely flowers which in the bud are dark red, brightening on opening. Healthy, vigorous and free. T.

Papa Meilland (sss). I hesitate to include this rose as one for beginners. A beautiful full flower, glowing red with deeper shadings, its growth leaves much to be desired. Subject to Mildew and very shy flowering. T.

PINK

Rose Pink

Eden Rose (s) (H). A vigorous, tough, trouble-free bush. The large flowers, deep rose pink shaded orange, are held erect well above strong deep green foliage. T.

Lively (sss) (H). A full deep rose pink of compact habit and very free flowering, making a first-class plant for bedding. S.

Bi-colour pinks

Femina. Striking in its fresh colour contrasts, salmon pink with silvery pink reflexes. The pointed flower unfolds its petals in shapely perfection. Tall in growth, a little less free in flower than one would like, it is nevertheless a rose of quality and character which deserves a place where good roses are grown. T.

Pink Favourite (ss) (H). A two-toned pink, soft shell pink within, salmon pink on the reverse. The large, shapely flowers are produced in great profusion, coming mostly three on a stem. If the two outer buds are removed a very large exhibition bloom results. The foliage is plentiful and the growth very free. An excellent bedding variety with few better. T.

Prima Ballerina (sss). A rose of distinguished refinement. The exquisite pointed, clear pink bloom is held gracefully erect on a wiry stem and is unaffected by adverse weather conditions. The foliage is healthy and abundant. Where a shorter rose is required this variety is to be strongly recommended. M.

Rose Gaujard (H). Of all trouble-free roses this holds pride of place. Of perfect health, its attractive glossy foliage is abundant, and the perfect foil for its large deep pink flowers with their silvery reverse, which open under the most adverse weather conditions. A rose bred for the 'wayfaring man' who though 'a fool' need not err in growing this accommodating rose. T.

Stella (s). Large, very full, deep peach-pink blooms. While I hesitate to include this as an easy rose to grow, results

GROUP 4: HYBRID TEA ROSES

can be so good that where exhibition size is required it is well worth trial and experiment. The growth is vigorous. T.

Pink and Gold

Astree (s) (H). Clear pink with a yellow base. The flower is attractive at all stages and withstands wet weather. The plant has everything to commend it—vigour, freedom, health—while the shapely flowers are produced in quantity with quality. T.

Helen Traubel (s) (H). Varying from pink in the long pointed buds to apricot in the full flower, which opens flat. Its only fault is its weak flower stem which causes the flowers to nod. Even so, one of the healthiest and most free flowering of bedding roses. T.

My Choice (sss) (H). The globular buds are yellow splashed scarlet, unfolding to clear pink with maize yellow reverse. A very easy and accommodating variety. Good for exhibition or bedding, its tall upright growth is free and healthy. Earlier than many sorts, it withstands wet weather and flowers until late autumn. T.

Clear Pink

Gavotte. A large, full flower of perfect shape. Useful for exhibition purposes. The foliage is strong, almost coarse, with vigorous upright growth. T.

Lady Sylvia (sss). A very old variety still grown in great quantities for forcing. Its soft pink is pleasing, especially in the autumn when its small blooms of exquisite shape are filled with fragrance and borne in great profusion. It is not vigorous by present-day standards and should be planted at 1 ft. 9 in. apart. S.

Michèle Meilland. Long pointed buds in clear mother-of-pearl shades. The many blossoms are held upright on wiry slender stems. Ideal for bedding or cutting. Easy to grow and most effective for display. M.

ORANGE-FLAME

Because most roses of salmon-orange colouring fade, many of the varieties enumerated could be classified as pink in their later stages.

Mischief. A very sturdy bushy plant carrying a number of full short-petalled flowers which often come 'quartered'. This in no way effects its bedding qualities which are excellent. The colour is crushed strawberry shaded orange.

Violinista Costa (H). A hardy variety of many years' standing. While the flowers are of no outstanding individual merit the over-all effect is extremely pleasing. The flowers are produced in great abundance in quick succession and the lovely glossy foliage makes an ornamental bed from May onwards. Because of its rapid growth extra sulphate of potash should be given in late August to replace food losses and mature the young wood for October flowering. The over-all colour is orange-flame, while the older flowers fade to salmon pink. M.

ORANGE GOLD

Super Star (ss) (H). Probably no garden should be without

GROUP 4: HYBRID TEA ROSES

this best-selling rose. The colour is unique, probably to call it intense golden vermilion gives some indication of it. Vigorous and healthy, it is a little slow in revealing its sterling qualities in the first season of planting. Once established it throws vigorous upright growths on the top of which are numerous short-stemmed flowers. It withstands adverse weather conditions and is extremely healthy. T.

Vienna Charm. Provided the soil conditions are good, this might be tried in industrial areas, when its proclivity to Mildew and Black Spot would be checked. Its unusually long ovoid buds open to immense flowers of golden-orange with an almost honey yellow sheen. At its best it is all rewarding—but you have been warned!

ORANGE SALMON

Diorama (s). A delightful multicolour with orange-yellow base splashed with orange-scarlet. The flowers are shapely, freely produced on tall upright stems springing from a healthy, well-foliaged plant. One of the best and most reliable of the newer bedding roses. M.

Mojave (H). A rose of mixed colouring, apricot-orange base with heavy veining of carmine. It has an upright growth of great freedom, carrying many flowers on wiry stems. Colourful, it is an extremely useful bedding variety which can yield an abundance of cut flowers over a long period. M.

Tapestry (H). A very attractive multi-coloured flower primarily for bedding. The colour of the flower and the glossy foliage combine to produce an excellent bush. M.

ORANGE YELLOW

Beauté (s). One of the most charming and graceful of roses. The flowers are rich apricot and are carried upright above a small but healthy plant. An ideal bedding plant. S.

Thais. Similar to the above in colour but with full rounded flowers on tall, upright stems. The foliage is strong and healthy. T.

YELLOW

Diana Menuhin. Intense golden yellow flowers carried on tall upright stems with deep green, glossy foliage. Useful for bedding. T.

Ellinor LeGrice (ss) (H). Globular buds opening to full, clear, unfading golden yellow, upright flowers. Opening in all weathers it provides a reliable hardy bedding rose. M.

Spek's Yellow. An old but reliable variety. Almost green buds which develop into small, deep golden yellow blooms, produced in great freedom, especially in the autumn when a single stem will carry a great candelabra of many flowers. T.

Summer Sunshine (s). The very large, rather loose, well shaped, deep golden flowers are carried on tall shoots on a vigorous shrub-like bush. Admirable for a tall specimen bush or low 5-ft. hedge. The foliage is handsome, plentiful and dark green. Should be watched for Black Spot. T.

GROUP 4: HYBRID TEA ROSES

Sutter's Gold (ss) (H). Rich orange-yellow shaded and veined with vermilion. The over-all effect is rich old gold. Delightful pointed blossoms, ideal for decoration either on the bush or for cut flowers. Remarkably healthy in growth and free with flower, it makes an ideal bedding rose. M.

CANARY YELLOW

Anne Watkins. Not an easy rose to place, for the clear but subdued tones might at times be classed in the buff pinks, and at other times as a pale yellow shaded apricot. But wherever placed it has many excellent qualities, freedom of shapely flower, resistance to wet, hardy and abundant growth. Its subdued colourings are an ideal foil for the harsh and over brilliant colours which are so difficult to place near less flaunting neighbours. M.

Dorothy Peach (H). This excellent rose suffers from being very similar in colour and form to Peace. Its growth is entirely different, being short and compact and therefore amenable to the companionship of normal growing roses. S.

Grandmère Jenny (H). A pointed shapely flower, graced with upright stem and handsome foliage. An excellent free flowering bedding rose in soft yellow with peach edging and shading. M.

Grandpa Dickson. Greenish ovoid buds opening into pale yellow flowers of exhibition form and substance. The growth is vigorous, upright and free. The old flowers spot badly in rain. At its best very good. Producing many high quality flowers. M.

King's Ransom (H). Probably the best of the clear, unfading yellow bedding roses. The flowers are well shaped, carried singly on vigorous upright stems, enhanced by abundant glossy foliage. Ideal for bedding and good for cutting.

Peace (H). More plants of this variety have been produced than any other rose. In a class by itself for vigour and health. The large full yellow flowers have varying degrees of carmine pink edging, partly varying with soils and climatic conditions. The flower is large to coarseness, but is particularly beautiful when full blown. In the first flowering a number of short shoots are produced without flowers. If these are left they will produce flowering shoots from their side growths. In bedding its vigour should be remembered. It makes a magnificent lightly pruned specimen bush and in this form may well be used among shrubs. T.

WHITE

Frau Karl Druschki (H). This old rose bears its flowers in a different fashion. producing a tall stem with a cluster of short-stemmed flowers at the top. The buds are sometimes stained red but the full bloom is pure dead white on opening. Suggested here as the only pure white with health. T.

Message. A typical, full blossom of the normal H.T. Rather shy in the production of flowers, these are of perfect form. Addicted to Mildew. M.

Pascali. Hardly pure white, for the centres of the blooms are shaded fawn and at times the buds lack clear defini-

GROUP 4: HYBRID TEA ROSES

tion. It is reasonably healthy and for this reason might well be endured where a white is required. M.

Virgo. Here is a lovely pure white bud which opens quickly into a flat, semi-double flower borne in great profusion. The short growth is upright and very free. It endures some rain quite cheerfully but is often spoiled by its weakness for Mildew. S.

Westfield Star (ss) (H). I have been taken to task for suggesting this very old rose, but it has freedom, hardiness and perfume. While not pure white—it has a pale lemon centre—the overall effect is there. S.

POLYCHROMES

Chicago Peace (H). A colour variation of 'Peace' with all the qualities of growth and flower, but with more intense colouring, as the pink has been changed into a deeper, more predominant carmine-scarlet staining. Somewhat variable, it will undoubtedly be improved by careful selection, when it should become very popular. T.

Piccadilly (H). Always in flower, producing an abundance of semi-double flowers, brilliant scarlet with golden reverse. A very showy bedding rose. M.

Tzigane. A more orthodox variety, with full flowers which are slightly globular. The growth is thorny, upright and free. M.

LILAC

Blue Moon (ss). A full bloom on a vigorous bush. Probably the best flower in its class but health is an uncertain quantity. M.

Heure Mauve. Not so shapely or perfumed as the above. The split blooms come freely on a healthy, upright bush and for this reason is to be recommended for bedding if such a colour is required.

Sterling Silver (sss). This is the earliest of this colour and is often much shown at exhibitions from forced blooms under glass. It is not easy to grow as the plants are rather weakly in the open and prone to disease.

Appendix

Selections for various purposes
This is an invidious task as difficult as choosing the winner at a baby show. The very limitation demands exclusion of some good varieties, but those selected have been chosen for ease of cultivation, variety of colour, and where two good varieties tie, perfume has been the deciding factor. Full descriptions are given on pages 106–142.

6 Ramblers, once flowering
    Albertine, salmon pink (p. 106)
    Chaplin's Pink, deep rose pink (p. 107)
    Crimson Shower, deep red, late flowering (p. 107)
    Emily Gray, old gold (p. 108)
    Paul's Scarlet, bright red (p. 108)
    Snowflake, pure white (p. 107)

6 medium Climbers or Ramblers flowering more than once
    Autumn Sunlight, golden-orange (p. 111)
    Danse de Feu, orange-scarlet (p. 111)
    Danse des Sylphes, bright red (p. 111)
    Golden Showers, yellow (p. 109)
    New Dawn, clear pink (p. 110)
    Pink Perpetué, bi-colour pink (p. 113)

6 tall Climbers
    Etoile de Hollande, deep red
    Lady Sylvia, clear pink (p. 112)
    Mme G. Staechelin, deep pink (p. 112)
    Mrs. Sam McGredy, coppery salmon (p. 113)

APPENDIX

Soldier Boy, single scarlet, perpetual (p. 114)
Super Star, golden orange (p. 136)

6 taller Bushes (H.T. type)
Ernest H. Morse, bright red (p. 132)
My Choice, pink with yellow reverse (p. 135)
Peace, yellow, tinged pink (p. 140)
Pink Favourite, bi-colour pink (p. 134)
Super Star, vermilion orange (p. 136)
Wendy Cussons, light red (p. 132)

6 shorter Bushes (H.T. type)
Blue Moon, slate blue (p. 142)
Champs Elysées, bright red (p. 132)
Chrysler Imperial, deep red (p. 133)
King's Ransom, clear yellow (p. 140)
Prima Ballerina, deep pink (p. 134)
Tapestry, orange-flame (p. 137)

6 taller Floribunda
Fervid, bright red (p. 121)
Goldgleam, yellow (p. 128)
Iceberg, white, (p. 129)
Pink Parfait, light and deep pink (p. 125)
Orange Sensation, orange yellow (p. 128)
Sweet Repose, pink and crimson (p. 124)

6 shorter Floribunda
Allgold, yellow (p. 128)
Chanelle, cream and pink (p. 124)
Circus, orange and peach (p. 126)
Lili Marlene, deep red (p. 122)
Plentiful, deep pink (p. 124)
Sarabande, bright red (p. 122)

Index

Aeration of soil, 22; treatment of consolidated beds, 38–9
Age attained by good rose, 43, 103
'American Pillar', rapid growth of, 75–6, 106
Anchor roots, 18, 19
Annual nettles, following use of poultry manure, 41
Aphides, varieties of, 70; *see* Pests
Artificial fertilizers, and organic, 39, 40; and watering, 82; *see* Humus
Asbestos sheet root barrier (protecting roses near hedges), 81

Beds for roses: allowing to consolidate, 27; preparing soil and digging new, 25–7, 29, 30; shapes and sizes, 25; renewing of, for one or several plants, 35–6; tidying after planting, 38–9
Black netting, under hedge roses, 80, 84
'Black Spot' disease, 66, 67, 127, 128, 129, 130, 137, 138; sprays against, 68
Blooms, identification and treatment of, 87–144; cutting of (stem length, etc.), 97; shape and colour, 88–9; *see* Roses, named
Bonemeal, 25, 26, 27, 30, 36, 40
Briar stocks, 41–3
British Standards Institution recommendations, 99
'Buccaneer' grown as specimen, 118

'Bud' of rose bush at planting, 32
Budding described, 41–3
'Buff Beauty' musk rose, for hedging, 83–4
Bush roses: choosing and buying, 99–102; pruning of, 63–4; types, 91–4

'Canary Bird' for hedging, 83
Captan (Orthocide) against 'Black Spot', 68
Caterpillars and grubs, 70–1; systemic poisons against, 70
'Chicago Peace', 12
'Chinatown' for hedging, 83
Chlorosis (iron deficiency), 71
Climbers: basic difference from ramblers, 90; description of three types, choice of, 110–14; old and new compared, 90–1; perpetual, for hedging, 84; resuscitation of old, 74–5; tying of, 75; some pruning methods, 58–9
Colour: fading, as bad fault, 94–5; history of changes in, 87–8
Compost, 22, 36, 39
Container-grown roses, 30
Copper sulphate, spraying with, 65–6
'Cornelia' musk rose, for hedging, 83–4
Corrugated iron, disadvantage of, 80–1
'Cuckoo-spit', 72
Cultivation programme, 38–43

INDEX

Cultivators, hiring of hand, 24
'Cushioning' of permanent stems, 79

'Dainty Maid' for hedging, 83; grown as specimen, 118
D.D.T.: against leaf-cutting bee, 72; against sawflies, 71; with Malathion, against greenfly, 70
Digging depth, for new beds, 25-6
'Diorama', 12
Diseases, 65-73; resistance against, 131-41
Di-Trapex, as fresh earth for new roses, 36
D.N.O.C. sprays, 70
Dormancy: and planting, or transplanting, 20, 32, 34; pruning to dormant eye, 49-53
Drainage, 21, 22, 23
Draughts, as cause of Mildew, 21
Dried blood, dangers of using, 40
Drying-out of roses before planting, 33, 34

Edges of beds, 25, 32
'Ellen Manny', 12
'Ena Harkness', 101; *see also* Roses, named
Epsom salts, against Mildew, 69
'Ernest H. Moore', 12
Exhibiting roses, 95-8

Fan training, 57, 74
Farmyard manure, 22, 30, 39; caution on origin of, 40; trace elements in, 40-1
'Femina', 12
Fencing of garden, 80-1
'Fervid' as red rose for hedges, 83
Fibrous roots, role of, 17, 18, 19, 29, 38
Fillis, for tying, 79
Floribunda: definition of class, 91; two types of, 91-2; cutting flowers from, 97; H.T. types, 92; pruning of, 60-2; choice of, for beginners, 124-30; *by colour:* bicolour and mixed, 130; mauves, 129; oranges, 126-7, 128; pink, 123-6; red, 121-3; white, 129; yellow, 128
Flower-head removal, 82
Flower spacing on truss, 95
Flower structure, 18
Flowering: key to successful, 74; two main types of, 88-9
Foliage of exhibition plants, 96
Forking over beds, danger of, 38
'Fred Loads' for hedging, 83
'Fresh earth' defined, 35
Froghoppers, spraying with Rogor against, 72
Frost, 33, 34, 38; and suckering, 43

'Gavotte', 12
Gloves: for pruning, 54; for spraying, 66
'Grandpa Dickson', 12
Grassing down of heavy soils, 21
Greenfly, 70; hosing down with jet of water, 81
'Guard eyes', rubbing away of, 82

Heavy soils, preparation of, 21-2
Hedge roses, risk of buying cheaply, 83; planting and pruning, 83-4
Hedges, fences: corrugated iron, 80-1; plastic netting, 80, 84; rose, 83-4; wattle, 80
'Heeling in' of newly arrived rose plants, 34
Hoeing, dangers of, 39
Hoof-and-horn, 40
Hose for watering, careful use of, 81
Housing-site soils, preparation of, 23
Humus, 22, 39, 41
Hybrid teas (H.T.s): defined, 93-4; how to cut flowers of, 97; *choice by colour grouping:* canary yellow, 139; dark red, 133; glowing red,

INDEX

Hybrid teas—*cont.*
132; lilac, 142; orange-flame, 136; orange-gold, 136-7; orange-salmon, 137; orange-yellow, 138; pinks (various), 133-6; pinky red, 131-2; polychromes, 141; white, 140-1; yellow, 138; pruning, 63-4

'Iceberg' as white hedge rose, 83
'Incense', 12
Industrial areas: 'Black Spot' kept in check in, 67; 'Copper Delight' in, 126; 'Paddy McGredy' in, 125; 'Vienna Charm' in, 137

John Innes compost as 'replacement earth', 36

Karathane (Dinocap) against Mildew, 69
Keserite against Mildew, 69
Knife *versus* secateurs for pruning, 53, 54
'Knock-down' weed killers, 27-8
'Knot' at junction of shoot and root, 32, 34
Kordes, Wilhelm, perpetual ramblers introduced by, 90; Kordesii group, pruning of, 58; choice of, 90, 91, 108-10

'Lady Sonia' for hedges, 83
Larch poles for stakes, pergolas: disadvantages of, 80
Lattices, treatment of against weather, 36-7
Leaf-cutting bee, 72
Le Grice, E. B., *Rose Growing Complete*, 22
Life-span of well-grown rose bush, 43, 103
Lime, excess of, from mushroom manure, 41
Loams, 22

Malathion, against sawflies, 71
Maneb, against 'Black Spot' and 'Rust', 68
Manuring, 39-41; compound rose manures, 40
'Message', 12
Mildew, 21, 66, 69; and temperature variations, 81; treatments against, 69; *see also* 'Frensham', 122, Polyantha roses, 130, 'Virgo', 141
'Mischief', 12
Mulching, 41
Mushroom manure, 41
Musk roses for hedging, 83-4
'My Choice', 12

Nitrogen, danger of excessive, 40, 41
North of England Horticultural Society grounds, Harlow Car, 105

'Old-fashioned' and shrub roses, 91; and species roses, choice of, 115-17
'Orange Sensation' for hedging, 83
Organic manures, 22, 39-41; composts, 22, 36, 39
Overfeeding, 39-40, 47
Overspraying, 66

'Peace' grown as specimen, 118
Peat, 22, 25, 26, 27, 30, 36, 39; function of, 21, 39, 41
Pergolas, 36-7; treatments of, against wind and weather, 36-8, 80
Perpetual climbers, pruning of, 59
Perpetual ramblers, 58, 90, 91, 108-10
Pests and diseases, 65-73
Petal quality, 89, 94
Phosphates, potash, nitrogen: proportions of, in rose manure, 40
Plant Varieties Act, 101-3

INDEX

Planting, 29–37; distances apart, 31; feeding of young bushes, 39, 40; general method, 30–1; informal, with 'lone' rose, 28; other arrangements, 25; 'staggered', 31–3; staking of standard, 36–7; some special points: dormant season, 20, 32, 34; resuscitation of shrivelled plants, 33; shortening of spreading growth, 38, 50; soaking, 33

Ploughing of housing site land, 23–4

Polyantha group, 91, 130; pruning of, 60–2

Post, training rose round, 57

Poultry manure, 41

'Prosperity' musk rose for hedging, 83–4

Pruning, 47–64; objects of, key to, 47–8; of bush H.T.s, 63–4; of climbers, 57, 59; of roses generally, good and bad cuts illustrated, 52–3; hard for first-year bushes, 50; for health, 50–1; of hedge roses, 62, 82, 83; of old but vigorous bushes, 51–2; of old-fashioned roses, shrubs, species, 60; of polyantha and floribunda, 60–2; of ramblers (three types), 56–8; 'summer', 54, 55; of weeping standards, 78

'Queen Elizabeth' for hedges, 83; as specimen, 118

Queen Mary Rose Garden, London, 105

Ramblers: types 1 and 2 described, 56–8, 89, 106–8; Kordesii and other perpetuals, 108–10; old and new, 89–90; introduction of perpetual, 90; perpetuals for hedging, 84; standards for (minimum sizes), 101, 103; on banks, 77; weeping, 77–8; flowering on, 12-months-old wood, 76; pruning of, 56–8

Replacement guarantees, 103

Resuscitation before transplanting, 33

Roath Park, Cardiff, 105

Rogor spray: against froghoppers, 72; against greenfly, 70

Root, 17–43; function, system, 17–19; stock, 18; of newly-delivered autumn plants, 29; shortening at time of planting, 29; to protect, at time of planting, 33

Rose slug worm, 72

Roses, named, with descriptions and notes on treatment (C: climbers of 3 sorts; F: floribundas; H.T.: hybrid teas; K: Kordesii; O: older varieties and species; P: perpetual ramblers; R: ramblers; S: shrubs):
'Africa Star' (F), 129
'Albéric Barbier' (R), 106
'Albertine' (R), 106, 143
'Allgold' (F), 111, 128
'Aloha' (C), 111
'Altissimo' (P), 109
'American Pillar' (R), 106
'Anna Wheatcroft' (F), 126
'Anne Watkins' (H.T.), 139
'Astrée' (H.T.), 135
'Autumn Sunlight' (C), 111, 143
'Ballerina' (S), 118
'Beauté' (H.T.), 138
'Blanc Double de Coubert' (O), 115
'Blue Moon' (H.T.), 142
'Bonn' (S), 118
'Buff Beauty' (S), 118
'Canary Bird' (O), 116
'Cardinal de Richelieu' (O), 116
'Casino' (C), 111
'Cécile Brunner' (O), 116
'Centifolia cristata' (O), 116
'Champs Elysées' (H.T.), 132
'Chanelle' (F), 124

INDEX

'Chaplin's Pink' (R), 107, 143
'Chaplin's Pink Companion' (R), 108
'Chicago Peace' (H.T.), 141
'Chrysler Imperial' (H.T.), 133
'Circus' (F), 126
'City of Leeds' (F), 123
'Crimson Glory' (C), 111
'Crimson Shower' (R), 107, 143
'Copper Delight' (F), 126
'Dainty Maid' (F), 123
'Dairy Maid' (F), 129
'Danse de Feu' (C), 111, 143
'Danse des Sylphes' (C), 108, 111, 143
'Dearest' (F), 125
'Diana Menuhin' (H.T.), 138
'Dimples' (F), 129
'Diorama' (H.T.), 137
'Dorothy Peach' (H.T.), 139
'Dr. Van Fleet' (R), 108
'Dusky Maiden' (F), 121
'Eden Rose' (H.T.), 133
'Elizabeth of Glamis' (F), 123
'Ellen Mary' (HT), 133
'Ellinor Le Grice' (C), 111; (H.T.), 138
'Emily Gray' (R), 108, 143
'Ena Harkness' (C), 111; (H.T.), 132
'Ernest H. Morse' (H.T.), 132
'Etoile de Hollande' (C), 143
'Europeana' (F), 121
'Evelyn Fison' (F), 121
'Excelsa' (R), 107
'Femina' (H.T.), 134
'Fervid' (F), 121
'Firecrest' (F), 122
'First Choice' (S), 118
'Flaming Sunset' (C), 112
'Fragrant Cloud' (H.T.), 131
'François Juranville' (R), 107
'Frau Karl Druschki' (H.T.), 140
'Fred Loads' (S), 118
'Frensham' (F), 122
'Gavotte' (H.T.), 135

'Gloire de Dijon' (C), 112
'Gold Marie' (F), 128
'Golden Dawn' (C), 112
'Golden Showers' (P), 109, 143
'Golden Slippers' (F), 127
'Golden Treasure' (F), 128
'Goldgleam' (F), 128
'Grand'mère Jenny' (H.T.), 139
'Grandpa Dickson' (H.T.), 139
'Guinée' (C), 112
'Helen Traubel' (H.T.), 135
'Heure Mauve' (H.T.), 142
'High Noon' (C), 112
'Iceberg' (F), 129
'Innisfree' (F), 125
'King's Ransom' (H.T.), 140
'Konrad Adenauer' (H.T.), 132
'Korona' (C), 112; (F), 127
'Lady Sonia' (S), 118
'Lady Sylvia' (C), 112; (H.T.), 135, 143
'Leverkusen' (K), 109
'Lilac Charm' (F), 129
'Lili Marlene' (F), 122
'Lively' (H.T.), 133
'Maigold' (P), 109
'Ma Perkins' (F), 124
'Marlena' (F), 122
'Masquerade' (C), 112; (F), 130
'Meg' (C), 112
'Mermaid' (P), 109
'Message' (H.T.), 140
'Meteor' (F), 122
'Michèle Meilland' (H.T.), 136
'Minnehaha' (R), 107
'Mischief' (H.T.), 136
'Mme G. Staechelin' (C), 112–13, 143
'Mme Laperrière' (H.T.), 133
'Mme Pierre Oger' (O), 116
'Mojave' (H.T.), 137
'Moyesii Geranium' (O), 117
'Mrs Sam McGredy' (C), 113, 143
'My Choice' (H.T.), 135
'New Dawn' (P), 108, 110, 143

INDEX

Roses—*cont.*
  'Numéro Un' (H.T.), 132
  'Orange Sensation' (F), 128
  'Paddy McGredy' (F), 125
  'Paintbox' (F), 130
  'Papa Meilland' (H.T.), 133
  'Parade' (C), 113
  'Park Director Riggers' (KP), 110
  'Pascali' (H.T.), 140
  'Paul's Scarlet', and P.S. 'Blaze Superior' (R), 108, 143
  'Peace' (C), 113; (H.T.), 140
  'Pernille Poulsen' (F), 124
  'Piccadilly' (H.T.), 141
  'Pink Favourite' (H.T.), 134
  'Pink Parfait' (F), 125
  'Pink Perpetue' (C), 113, 143
  'Plentiful' (F), 124
  Polyanthas and Poulsen Type Hybrid Polyanthas (F), 130
  'Posy' (F), 124
  'Prima Ballerina' (H.T.), 134
  'Princess Michiko' (F), 127
  'Queen Elizabeth' (F), 126
  'Ritter Von Barmstede' (KP), 110
  'Roger Lamberlin' (O), 117
  'Rose Gaujard' (H.T.), 134
  'Royal Gold' (C), 113
  'Rubrifolia' (O), 117
  'Salmon Sprite' (F), 125
  'Sarabande' (F), 122
  'Scarlet Queen Elizabeth' (F), 122
  'Scented Air' (F), 126
  'Schneezwerg' (O), 117
  'Sea Pearl' (F), 125
  'Shepherdess' (F), 130
  'Shot Silk' (C), 113
  'Snowflake' (R), 107, 143
  'Soldier Boy' (C), 114
  'Spek's Yellow' (C) 114); (H.T.), 138
  'Stella' (H.T.), 134
  'Sterling Silver' (H.T.), 142
  'Summer Sunshine' (H.T.), 138
  'Super Star' (H.T.), 136
  'Sutter's Gold' (H.T.), 139
  'Sweet Repose' (F), 124
  'Sweet Sultan' (C), 114
  'Tapestry' (H.T.), 137
  'Telstar' (F), 130
  'Thais' (H.T.), 138
  'Tzigane' (H.T.), 141
  'Veilchenblau' (R), 107
  'Versicolor' ('Rosa Mundi') (O), 117
  'Vesper, (H.T.), 127
  'Vienna Charm' (H.T.), 137
  'Violinista Costa' (H.T.), 136
  'Virgo' (H.T.), 141
  'Wendy Cussons' (H.T.), 132
  'Westfield Star' (H.T.), 141
  'William Allen Richardson' (C), 114
  'Woburn Abbey' (F), 127, 128
  'Zambra' (F), 127
Rotovators, 24
Rotting in the bud, 94
Row planting, for colour mass, 31
Royal Horticultural Society's gardens, Wisley, 105
Royal National Rose Society's grounds, St. Alban's, 105
'Rubbing away', excess 'eyes', 82
Rugosa hybrids for hedging, 83
'Rust', 67, 68; *see* 'Dearest', 125

Sandy soils, 22
Sawflies, 71–2
Scent, choosing for, 115–42
Seaweed as fertilizer, 39
Seeding of roses, 19
'Shattering' defined, 95
Shoddy, use of, 40
Shoot, 47–84; function of, 19; three stages of season's growth, 47; 'blind shoots', 71; distinguishing between shoots and suckers, 43

INDEX

Shortening: of growth, at planting time, 38; of root, at planting time, 29; of plant, against autumn windrock, 54; distinct from pruning, 50
Shrub roses, some suggested, 118–19; pruning of, 60
Sisal, for tying, 79
Site planning, 24–5
Soaking before planting, 33
Soils, 21–3; improving and preparing, 25–7; condition of, at planting time, 27; old rose soil useless for new roses, 35, 36; firmness and texture of, 38–9
'Sporting', 90–1
Sprays, 24, 27, 40, 65; methods and frequency of applying, 65; precautions when using, 66; systemic, 70
Spring pruning, 49, 50
'Staggered' planting, 31–3
Stakes, 78; making and treating, 80; using at planting time, 36–7; and wind damage, 38
Standard rose, B.S.I. definition of, 99
Stony soils, 22
Subsoil, enriching the, 26–7
Suckers, 20; from old stock after budding, 42–3; danger of cutting instead of pulling out, 43
Sucking and leaf eating insects, 70
Sulphate of potash: autumn use of, 40, 136; for wood hardness, 67
Sulphur (green) against Mildew, 69
Summer pruning, 54–5

Tarred string, for tying, 79
'Tea' roses, 93
'Thais', 12
'Tipping' of old-fashioned roses, 91
Tomato manure for roses, 40
Top soil: extra, for newly planted roses, 27, 29, 33; improving shallow, gravelly, chalky, 23
Trace elements, 40
Training, staking, tying, 74–80
Trellis, making and preserving, 80

'Uncle Walter', grown as specimen, 101, 118

'Vienna Charm', 12
Vine eyes, use of, 80
Virus, 'Masquerade' as carrier of, 130

Watering: of climbers, ramblers, near wall, 36, 37, 82; of newly-planted roses, 30, 31; general rules of, 81–2
Wattle fencing, 80
Weed-killing sprays, 24, 27; residues of, in farmyard manure, 40
Weeping (standard) ramblers, 77–8, 106
'Wendy Cusson', 12
Windrock, 32, 38, 54
Winds, drying, at planting time, 33
Wire, avoidance of for tying, 79
Wood: choice of, for stakes, pergola, etc., 80
Woody growth: renewal of, removal of, 50, 51, 60, 62